LIFE AFTER EMOTIONALLY IMMATURE PARENTS

RECOVERING FROM UNHEALTHY CHILDHOOD
ATTACHMENTS, BREAKING THE HARMFUL CYCLE &
RECLAIMING YOUR LIFE WITH 8 TECHNIQUES TO
FORM SECURE ATTACHMENTS

VANESSA A. P.

D1607649

CONTENTS

I dedicate this book to anyone who may have experienced trauma, I know you are braver than you think.

A special thanks to my family and friends, especially my wonderful daughters and my husband for showing me that my "dream family" was possible.

STAY ON TOP!

I invite you to like my social media accounts so you can stay on top of content on this subject and follow the launch of future books.

Facebook group: Emotionally Immature Parents - Helping each other to Break the Toxic Cycle

My Facebook page: Vanessa A. P. Author

My Instagram page: vanessa.ap.author

FOREWORD

Since my graduation, I've always been interested in family relationships, especially the relationship between parents and their children. For me, it all started with a simple question, "Who are the main references for a child?" In case you don't know the answer, I'll make it easy for you: it is their parents and/or primary caregivers (depending on family configuration). When explaining like that, it seems obvious, however, in practice not so much. This subject always intrigues me because we know parenting is a determinant factor in developing children's personalities, and they can be a good or a bad reference for them.

Based on this question, I've decided to study ways to establish an assertive relationship between parents and their children, to consequently have them become healthy adults.

As a psychologist, I constantly come across people in my office who criticize themselves: they criticize their appearance, choices, and attitudes. When I try to understand the reason for this behavior, I realize that, in many cases, there are internalized critical parents. This may be just one of the thousands of symptoms arising from emotionally dysfunctional parents. My main goal as a professional is to help my patients to find tools to break this behavior cycle. My main goal as a person is to stop repeating this cycle.

Throughout her own experience, Vanessa elucidates that to be a good parent, you don't need to be perfect, just emotionally mature enough to recognize your responsibilities. First, you will realize that you are not alone. Second, you will learn to identify dysfunctional behaviors and, finally, most importantly, realize that it is possible to break a toxic cycle.

For those who don't know, Vanessa is the mother of two beautiful girls. I have the privilege of following them closely and, I can say, she has been amazing in recognizing her daughters' basic needs and, above all, her responsibility in this entire process.

You may feel emotionally touched reading this book. You might remember and associate it with difficult times you have experienced or recognize certain behavior cycles in your family circle. But Vanessa will welcome you and show that you can make a difference and stop repeating the same toxic cycle.

You are not alone,

Amanda Vidal - Psychologist

INTRODUCTION

Did you suffer from the effects of having emotionally immature parents?
Are you looking to stop the trauma cycle from defining who you are?
Do you have kids now, and you want to make sure you don't repeat the same emotional abuse your parents inflicted on you?

This is how many children of emotionally unavailable and/or narcissistic parents feel. People who have endured this type of situation have long-lasting effects throughout their life. Immature parents try to paint themselves as the victims in all situations and this leads the children to have to act like adults. You may have found that you spent your childhood caring for your parents and their emotional needs instead of the other way around. Now, you may have your own children to care for, and you want to be sure that this cycle is not repeated.

Having personal experience in this area, I can assure you that what you are going through matters deeply to me. I am someone who has been there! I lived with my grandmother until I was 12 years old. Afterward, I moved in with my mother and stepfather. This is when everything changed for me. Now, I am a mother of two girls and I realized the need for other parents like myself to be conscious of their childhood in order to be able to break the vicious cycle. The contents of this book helped me to personally break the emotional abuse cycle and I am certain it will also help people who have been in the same kind of situation.

You may wonder, how do I know if my parents were truly emotionally unavailable? We will discuss the traits and behaviors of emotionally unavailable parents and how your childhood may have looked. Acknowledging this aspect of your younger life will be no easy task. You may have to relive some painful memories and recognize the aspects of your parents that have had a lasting impact on you.

It's natural for many adults who were *emotionally abused* as a child to deny the reality of their situation.

They may even carry guilt and shame for years, assuming that every time their parents said, "It's your fault!" it was the truth. However, we will uncover critical psychological terms such as **gaslighting** and **projection** in an effort to highlight the true nature of your parents' manipulation. The signs and symptoms of emotional abuse can sometimes go undetected for years, and we will highlight all the ways they can manifest so you will be able to assess which of them most closely align with your personal experience. This book will help you recognize this emotional abuse cycle and how you may have been trapped in it for years.

Another common question is, *but why do I still feel guilty and even sympathize with my parents?* This phenomenon is due to **trauma bonding**, which is when a victim of abuse actually bonds with their abuser.

Handling emotionally unavailable parents is taxing enough, but once you have your own children, you must take the responsibility for having a healthy relationship with them. This is the same responsibility that your parents were unable to take within their relationship with you. For me, this was a frightening concept. I feared that I would be unable to be a better parent to my child than my parents were to me. I did not want to make my girls feel the way that I used to feel. These worries will all be addressed in the coming chapters.

We will talk about how you can take the steps to be an emotionally available parent to your child and how this does not mean you have to be perfect all the time! We are all human, but a child can feel whether you are emotionally available or not. And once you become a parent, it is a priority to make your child feel heard and secure emotionally with you.

Rising above childhood trauma is not easy. But once you have children of your own, there is no other choice but to do so. Your parents may never change, as they have become masters at making everything about them. However, you have the ability to create a healthy, happy relationship with your children. Throughout the coming chapters, we will learn how our parents influenced our life, how to break the trauma cycle, and the steps of healing going forward.

VANESSA A. P.: AUTHOR BIO

Vanessa A. P. is a nutritionist, mother, and the author of *Life After Emotionally Immature Parents.*

Her work tackles the subject of healing from emotional abuse and breaking the cycle of trauma, and it is built on her own healing journey. Having lived happily with her grandmother until she was 12 years old, Vanessa spent her teenage years in a complex new dynamic with her mother and stepfather. She later came to understand that the route of her problems was the emotional unavailability of her parents, and their behavior had ramifications on her life for many years to come. Once she became a parent herself, Vanessa felt compelled to address her past issues in order to make sure she was the mother she wanted to be to her daughters.

Vanessa has studied and researched emotional abuse extensively, combining everything she's learned with her own therapy and life experience to produce a guide aimed at helping children of emotionally immature parents to live a full and happy life, free from the damage caused to them in childhood. She focuses on breaking the cycle so that harmful behaviors are left in the past and are not passed onto future generations.

Vanessa is of the firm belief that what happened to you in the past does not have to frame your future, and she's determined to help others achieve the peace and clarity she's found for herself.

Vanessa lives with her husband and two young daughters, with whom she would happily spend all her time if she could. She loves dogs and is constantly inspired by the unconditional love and emotional openness they offer us every day.

1

THE ONLY WAY FOR CHILDREN TO BE CHILDREN IS WHEN THEIR PARENTS ARE ADULTS

When we think of a child, we often think of a human being still in the developmental stages of childhood. They are between birth and puberty. They are also referred to as minors, as they have less responsibility than adults and cannot yet make important decisions. They must legally be under the care of a parent or another responsible caregiver. This simple definition of a child reflects that they cannot possibly take on the role of an adult. However, with emotionally immature parents, this is what often happens. Children are blamed, neglected, and emotionally abused, all because their parents are unwilling to take responsibility. This can have a lasting effect, as childhood is when much of our development processes take place physically, mentally, and emotionally.

TRAUMA & DEVELOPMENT

Many of us are familiar with **PTSD *or post-traumatic stress disorder***, which is often experienced by those who have been exposed to extreme traumatic situations. We see this in many war veterans as they have to adapt to life-threatening situations. Once they return home, they may have a hard time adjusting to regular life. A disorder that is less known is one that many children experience after growing up in environments filled with abuse, instability, and neglect. This is called ***Developmental Trauma Disorder***.

Developmental Trauma Disorder: *A disorder that develops after prolonged exposure to stress and adverse experiences; continues long after the experiences stop* (Shore, 2019).

Whenever we are exposed to threatening situations, our bodies release the stress hormone cortisol. Prolonged threatening situations create anxiety, agitation, and hyper-vigilance. *This is devastating to a child's growth because this chronic response alters the developmental process.* The brains and bodies of children grow differently due to the trauma, as their sense of themselves and the world becomes flipped. Parents are supposed to be the ones to take care of us, emotionally and physically. When this does not happen, children develop feelings of distrust, guilt, and fear. There is no way for them to understand that their parents' inability to take responsibility is not their fault.

WHAT IS AN EMOTIONALLY IMMATURE PARENT?

In order to have strong emotional maturity and emotional intelligence, one must have self-awareness, empathy, and self-regulation. This is a primary component to healthy, lasting relationships. On the other hand, emotional immaturity is often the result of insecure attachments, trauma, addictions, mental health problems, or an inability to work on oneself. Having a parent who is emotionally immature is frustrating and often leads to a negative relationship. Read through the following list and see which signs ring true about your parents:

- *They are egocentric.*
- *They do not have empathy.*
- *They are emotionally insensitive.*
- *They fear feelings and teach you that certain feelings are bad.*
- *They respond to happiness or joy negatively.*

- *They have no respect for different opinions.*
- *They do what benefits them the most.*
- *They cannot handle stress.*
- *They are very defensive.*
- *They blame others for their faults/mistakes.*

This is only a brief list and in the next chapter, we will go over some other expectations your emotionally immature parents may have inflicted upon you. Because this type of parent uses the same playbook, they often use similar language to put down their children or make the situation about them. If you experienced any of the above, you may now have the following symptoms:

- *Unhappy feelings and guilt surrounding those feelings*
- *Difficulty trusting yourself and other people*
- *Low self-worth and confidence*
- *Feeling trapped in the relationship with your parents*
- *Being highly sensitive*

Because you may have been constantly told you were wrong, as an adult you may now find it difficult to trust in your own instincts and intuition. You may have also felt extremely lonely, even when in the presence of your parents. This is because your emotional needs were never acknowledged or met. You might be thinking, well, my experience wasn't that bad! I shouldn't complain. So many victims of emotional abuse think this way, but having your physical needs met as a child is not enough. Parents must provide a safe environment for a child emotionally and mentally, as well as physically.

FOUR TYPES OF IMMATURE PARENTS

1. **Overly Emotional**: This parent's entire life is run by their feelings. If they are happy, sad, or angry, everyone around them must know it and react to it. They may overreact to small inconveniences, acting as if it is the end of the world. Most of the time, this type of parent needs external factors to calm themselves down. This may include other people or substances to alleviate their emotions. Many overly emotional parents are addicts and create a very unstable environment for their children. They swing back and forth between a strong involvement with their child to wanting nothing to do with them. This is confusing and harmful for the child, as they won't be able to

understand that this behavior has nothing to do with them and they often feel guilty, assuming they did something wrong for their parents to act this way. Children often understand more than they are given credit for, and they will absorb the parent's emotions, taking them on without fully understanding their meaning.

2. **Driven**: This parent may appear to be highly involved in their child's life. However, they are also controlling to the point where they interfere in their child's development, preventing them from making any decisions or mistakes and taking away from opportunities for learning and growth. This does not allow for any true emotional connection to form, as this parent-child relationship is more about control than anything else. It is goal-oriented and compulsive. Driven parents expect the child to want the same things at all times. Without the separation of two selves, there is the threat of a *codependent* attachment forming. This type of unhealthy attachment will be discussed in Chapter Six.

3. **Passive**: Passive parents do not want to "deal" with anything upsetting. They will be the favorite parent because they do not implement

any discipline. However, this means there is no guidance or parental boundaries in place. Children do not learn how to act appropriately in social situations. They may appear to lack manners when they are in school or with friends. The child does not learn anything from this parent and no connection can build out of such a relationship. This parent will allow their partner to do all the work and may even allow for neglect or abuse out of fear of having to deal with the real work. If their child does come to them with real feelings or a real problem, this parent may diminish or minimize the situation altogether.

4. **Rejecting**: This parent has no interest in being a parent. They are busy with other activities, as everything revolves around them. Maybe they are busy engaging in substance abuse or have a busy social agenda that does not involve the children. The family knows not to bother or upset this parent. They will not engage with the children in any meaningful way and the only time they do will be to yell or give a command. This parent will further distance themselves if others in the family attempt to get closer emotionally because the closeness makes them

uncomfortable. This will hinder a child's emotional growth and teach them that their feelings are not as important or relevant as the parent's feelings.

THE NARCISSISTIC PARENT

The above four types of emotionally immature parents are the most common; however, there is one type which deserves its own category: *the narcissistic parent*. This parent has narcissistic personality disorder, one of the many different types of personality disorders.

Narcissistic personality disorder (NPD): *an inflated sense of their own importance, a deep need for excessive attention and admiration, troubled relationships, and a lack of empathy for others* (Mayo Clinic).

Underneath this mask is actually a very fragile self-esteem. Narcissists cannot handle any criticism because they do not want it to affirm their worst fears about not being good enough. Boundaries are a big problem, as they do not respect the boundaries of anyone around them. They want what they want and they want it now! Manipulation is also a primary tactic, as they will do anything to get what they need in the moment. Sadly, children quickly learn how to adapt to what the narcissist wants. They comply and refrain from complaining out of fear of their parents withdrawing their affection. *Does this sound familiar?* Having a narcissistic parent has often been compared to walking on eggshells, as children try to delicately tiptoe around them, avoiding setting them off. Some specific signs of a narcissistic parent include:

- *Poor boundaries*
- *Acting like you're a burden*
- *Being antagonistic*
- *Lack of consistency*
- *Superiority*
- *Lack of empathy*
- *Jealousy of your accomplishments*
- *Neglectfulness*
- *Manipulation*

In Chapter Three, we will discuss emotional abuse and manipulation, and several specific tactics that emotionally immature parents inflict upon their children. It is possible that your parents were really victims of their own parents, and their parents were also victims. This is how the toxic cycle continues through generations. *But remember, the only person responsible for your failures or successes in your life is YOU.* The same applies to your parents. Though they may have tried and may still try to blame their failures or mistakes on you, only they are at fault for their own shortcomings. Their problems were already there long before you arrived, so you are not the problem and it is not your fault. Your parents may have even tried to tell you that you have ruined their life, in turn attempting to blame you for their choice to have a child. This is nonsense! We are all responsible for our own choices and you have made the right one to take control of your life by breaking the trauma cycle and learning how to have a healthy relationship with your own children.

CHAPTER SUMMARY

- A disorder that is lesser known than PTSD is one that many children experience after growing up in environments filled with abuse, instability, and neglect. This is called *developmental trauma disorder*.
- Emotional immaturity is often the result of insecure attachments, trauma, addictions, mental health problems, or an inability to work on oneself. Having a parent who is emotionally immature is frustrating and often leads to a negative relationship.
- The four types of emotionally immature parents are overly emotional, passive, driven,

and rejecting. The narcissistic parent is another, more severe type.

In the next chapter you will learn why we often deny the reality of our parents' emotional immaturity and why we choose to do so.

2

DENIAL: THE PAINFUL TRUTH ABOUT YOUR PARENTS AND YOUR RELATIONSHIP

It is easier to deny emotional abuse than physical abuse because there are no bruises. But emotional abuse leaves scars that are not easily visible and this is how we lead ourselves and those around us to think that nothing is wrong. These scars are engraved into our souls and will stay there forever if we don't actively choose to acknowledge and heal them. Denying the painful truth about our parents only strips away our power to deal with the situation. This can make things more difficult for us later on, as we are more likely to end up with similar people in future relationships. Without recognizing the truth and the abuse now, we won't be able to do so in the future.

Denial carves a path for us to repeat the same situation over and over.

Believe me, I know how hard it is to permanently distance yourself from those who have caused pain. But it is worth it and you deserve to live a peaceful life in which you don't have to constantly fight back against emotionally abusive parents. Even now as an adult, you might still be unsure if you truly suffered emotional abuse. This is common because if the situation was not properly addressed, then you have become accustomed to it and to you, it is normal. However, there is also a deeper aspect. Those who have endured abuse often form a kind of attachment to their abuser. This is called a trauma bond.

TRAUMA BONDING TO EMOTIONALLY ABUSIVE PARENTS

This is a type of deep, psychological connection between a victim and their abuser. You might be thinking, *But I'm not a victim! It was only my parents.* If you were exposed to any of the parent types discussed in the previous chapter, then you certainly endured some kind of mental and/or emotional abuse. This trauma bonding happens when the victim develops sympathy for their abuser. This sympathy takes a varying amount of time to form in each individual situation. For some, it takes a few days and for others, several years.

Trauma Bond: A psychological response to abuse that occurs when the abused person forms an unhealthy bond with the person who abuses them (Johnson and Zoppi, 2020).

One well-known type of trauma bonding is **Stockholm syndrome**. This term came to be after an attempted bank robbery in Stockholm, Sweden in 1973. Employees at the bank were held hostage for six days. On the seventh day, they were rescued. *Interestingly enough, the hostages were actually defending those who kept them captive.* Some hostages refused to give testimony in court and others even collected money to help their defense! This type of trauma bonding is also found in abusive relationships. There are several conditions that must be present in order for Stockholm Syndrome to be accurately diagnosed.

1. **Perceived Threat**: The victim must feel a threat to their life. This threat does not have to be a physical one and within your relationship with your parents, it most likely was not physical. Usually, the threat you felt was to your mental and emotional self. You had to keep your emotions at bay and never show that you were upset. However, you were on high alert all the time around your parents, in an attempt to keep from upsetting them. Therefore, this fear is as real as any other. This makes the victim

question themselves and their own perception, wondering if they should actually be afraid or not. They doubt their own feelings toward the reality of the situation, which sets them up for the ultimate manipulation later on.

2. **Isolation**: It is easy for parents to isolate their children. After all, they are the guardians! They may keep them from joining sports teams, hanging out with friends or other family members, and engaging in any extracurricular activities. Once isolated, the parent becomes the child's only frame of reference. Everything they learn or don't learn about the world and communication comes from them. This also means they will not have anyone to rely on emotionally, as their parents are the only adults in their life. Without others, the child will never learn that the behavior of their parents isn't natural. They will assume that their experience is the same as that of other children and continue relating to other people in this manner throughout their growth.

3. **Perceived Inability to Escape:** Once isolated, children quickly realize that they have nowhere to escape to. The hostages in the Stockholm robbery did not know whether they would be saved or not. This created a sense of being

trapped. At first, they may have had strong hopes, but over time, those hopes started to dwindle away and they had to cope with the situation as it was. While dealing with emotional abuse, children may not know who to reach out to in order to get help. This can have a negative psychological impact, as they learn how to adapt to their parents' needs instead of living in a healthy environment. Similarly to the hostages, they might consider telling someone at first, but decide that the repercussions from the parent would be even worse and decide instead to stay quiet.

4. **"Sprinkling Kindness"**: The parent is not *always* abusive toward their children. You may think back on your childhood and say, *Well, it wasn't always bad!* This is actually a tactic to keep the victim trapped in the **emotional abuse cycle**, which we will discuss in depth in the next chapter. In the Stockholm robbery, the hostages were shown some kindness at some point. Maybe the captors gave them food or water and told them that everything would be fine. It's possible they even tried to justify the reasoning behind the robbery in the first place, making the hostages feel empathetic to them. This led them to believe that the captors were not

terrible people, even though they were keeping them hostage! This phenomenon is actually chemical, as our bodies react to the repeated trauma followed by kindness by releasing different chemicals that further bond us to the abuser. This chemical reaction is a way to keep us alive and help our minds stay sharp so that we can protect ourselves in the face of danger. This has a negative effect on children, as they are being constantly exposed to this chemical reaction, leaving them in a state of confusion and survival mode within their own home.

THE BIOCHEMICAL EFFECT OF THE TRAUMA BOND

The trauma endured within the abusive relationship with your parents has a biochemical element in which your body releases chemicals, making you further bond with the abuser. When your parents would show you kindness or any kind of affection, *dopamine* would be released.

Dopamine: *The chemical released when we eat food we enjoy, give in to other cravings, etc. It is responsible for boosting mood, emotional responses, and is often referred to as the "feel-good" transmitter* (Psychology Today).

This chemical operates in the pleasure center of our brains. With the constant uncertainty, "sprinkles" of kindness, and abuse, a drug-like addiction is created. This makes things very confusing for children, as they feel they are unable to disconnect from their immature and abusive parents even once they have entered adulthood. This is actually a cycle that can be damaging emotionally and mentally over time. You have likely been through this *abuse cycle* with your parents several times without being aware of it and it may still be going on in your adult years. In the next chapter, we will discuss this abuse cycle in depth, going through each part and thinking all the way back in your childhood to when the abuse may have started. This type of cycle needs to be repeated over and over again in order to ensure that the parent has control over the child. Many of you may have been completely unaware of this cycle, which is normal.

THE UNREALISTIC EXPECTATIONS OF THE EMOTIONALLY IMMATURE PARENT

In the previous chapter, we spoke of the common traits of an emotionally immature parent. You may have been able to connect and identify with several that are applicable to your own parents. While these traits were broader, these expectations will hit home. Often, our parents expect a great deal. Without the emotional maturity to be a true parent, much of the adult responsibility falls onto the child. This creates expectations for them to grow up quicker than they would have naturally and creates an environment where the child must please the parent in order to avoid being chastised. Let's take a look at some unrealistic expectations that your parents may have had for you:

1. Fear me but love me

You likely lived in constant fear of what mood your parents would be in. You were careful not to upset them, and even if you knew what their triggers were, sometimes they would fly off the handle on something new that you couldn't have possibly predicted. Therefore, you were forced to admire and love your parents in order to avoid being yelled at or criticized, making you live in constant apprehension of what could happen. This taught you that their feelings were more important than your own. Children have their own lives! You might have had trouble with friends or difficulty with your grades in school, yet when you came home, nothing was about you. You had to continue acting perfect or your troubles would continue.

2. You are an adult, but only when I say so

Emotionally immature parents have a tendency to overshare with their children or to put adult responsibilities onto them. The parent is the one who should be taking care of their issues. Many times, the parent will tell children inappropriate gossip or allow the child to believe certain negative situations are happening because it is their fault. Even when the parent doesn't insinuate a situation is the child's fault, the child may still take it that way because they cannot possibly understand all the complexities of the adult world. Not only this, but when the emotionally immature parent does not want to handle their adult responsibilities, they often put the stress of them on their children. Many children also take care of younger siblings or are the sole caretaker for the household. They cook, clean, do laundry, and sometimes even pay the bills. While it's good for children to learn some responsibility through a certain amount of household chores, children should not be doing most of the work.

3. You must be better than everyone else, but you can't be special

It is important for these types of parents to see their children be better than others. This is especially true for **narcissistic parents**, as their child is often an extension of their ego. The more their child succeeds, the better they feel about themselves. Usually, they pressure their children to be the best in school or extracurricular activities. Many children of narcissistic parents excel in sports as well and the parents will pay for private coaches, extra practice time, and anything else to help them get ahead. However, even when the child performs very well, they don't want their child to feel too special because then they would believe in themselves. The emotionally immature parent always makes sure the child grows up believing they are a disappointment. This way, they stay at the mercy of the parent.

4. Tell me everything, but I will use it against you

Your parents may have demanded to know everything about you. They want to know about what's going on with your grades, friends, or any romantic interests in your life. This likely made you feel uncomfortable, as your parents are regularly emotionally unavailable to share your feelings, yet they want to know all your secrets. You might have felt comfortable sharing with other people in your life, but not with them. This definitely upset them! They might have made you feel bad for sharing things with your friends or other family members with whom you felt more comfortable. So, you eventually gave in and told them. But once you told them, they used it against you and would put you down because of your feelings. Maybe you told them you were worried about a test, and they put you down for not studying harder. Maybe you told them about someone you liked in school and they told you that person would never date you. It is in this way that emotionally immature parents manipulate their children in an attempt to feel superior.

5. Do exactly what I say, but if you fail, it's your fault

Nothing was ever their fault! Your parents likely blamed you for anything that did not go well. This could have been school activities, sports, or relationships. They may have told you exactly what to do, yet when it failed, it was your fault. This is also often the case with the **narcissistic parent** and happens as a product of #3. This makes a child feel like they can't possibly succeed because even when they seemingly do everything right, it is still not good enough. Children make mistakes and as a matter of fact, all people make mistakes! But children should never be belittled or put down for trying something, especially something new, and failing. Doing so is one of the most important lessons in life, and parents should be there to help pick them back up and encourage them to try again. If not, children often carry unwarranted **shame and guilt** into their adulthood. This will be discussed more in Chapter Five.

6. *Get away from me, but never leave me*

It may have been a big deal when you finally moved out of your home. Emotionally immature parents *never* want this to happen. They may have pushed you away by saying you do not contribute enough, are lazy, etc. They likely made fun of you for still living at home, even when you were still a young adult and were trying to get into the workforce as we all do! But then, when you finally did get ready to move out, they turned it on you again by saying you were wasting money by renting somewhere else. *This is because no matter what you do, the emotionally immature parent will never be satisfied.* They are only satisfied when they have something to criticize. These parents do not want you to move out for two key reasons, they do not want you to have your own life and they do not want to lose their primary caretaker.

7. *Take my advice/help, but stop using me*

At some point in your childhood or early adulthood, your parents likely offered you help. This may have been in the form of money, food, clothes, etc. It could have also been in the form of advice or life advice. They may have done this out of necessity or because they wanted to use it as leverage later on. They also did this to make you feel safe. They were convincing and told you that you should accept what they are offering you. But once you did, they threw it back in your face, claiming that you are using or exploiting their generosity. It made you feel bad and once again you questioned your whole perception, wondering, *Am I taking advantage of them?* Parents should be there to help their children and offer advice and support. Not to mention, they must provide food, shelter, and clothes. You should not feel guilty for receiving these basic necessities from them, however frugal they may have been.

RECOGNIZING THE TRUTH

After reading through this chapter and the common unrealistic expectations of immature parents, you are likely realizing the true nature of your parents. It is exhausting to constantly fight back against their tactics, trying to prove to them that you are worthy when all they do is attempt to put you down in an effort to feel better about themselves. But in order for you to move forward in your own life, you must see your parents for who they truly are. The next chapter will further highlight the nature of your parents' tactics, but for now, it's okay to take a moment and recognize the truth. Validate your feelings and understanding of the situation. You may have known for years, even as a child, that you were being unfairly blamed, yelled at, and abused. This is your proof!

While we can't change the past, we can better understand it and learn how to break the cycle going forward. Toxic relationships, regardless of their nature (romantic, social, familial, or parental), are like a disease. They are extremely difficult to cure and even harder initially to recognize. Now that you are an adult, you can make your own rules for what is acceptable and what isn't in your life. This is when you can set **boundaries** and begin to implement them with your parents if they are still a part of your life. Either way, boundaries are a great way to ensure that your relationships are healthy and prosperous in the future. These boundaries will be discussed in Chapter Eight.

CHAPTER SUMMARY

- Denying the painful truth about our parents only makes us powerless to deal with the problem and we end up unable to recognize similar people in future relationships.

- Trauma bonding happens when the victim develops sympathy for their abuser. This sympathy takes a varying amount of time to form in each individual situation. For some, it takes a few days, and for others, several years.
- Without the emotional maturity to be a true parent, much of the adult responsibility falls onto the child. This creates expectations for them to grow up quicker than they would have naturally and creates an environment where the child must please the parent in order to avoid being chastised.

In the next chapter, you will learn what is considered emotional abuse and how the abuse cycle operates.

3

THE EMOTIONAL ABUSE CYCLE AND MANIPULATION TACTICS

A buse can be difficult to identify. It is not always as shocking as a physical bruise. Some forms of abuse are not as easily recognized. With certain types, such as verbal, mental, and emotional abuse, victims may go years with only a vague feeling that something is wrong. Specifically, *that something is wrong with them.* It's important to recognize that anyone can be a victim of abuse. Alternatively, anyone can be a perpetrator of abuse as well. Many people cannot recognize the abuse they are enduring due to a lack of healthy examples. If you had a childhood without healthy and loving relationships, especially with your parents, then abuse may feel normal to you. Victims of abuse internalize the abuse and *believe there is something wrong with them, instead of something wrong with how they are being treated.*

The definition of emotional abuse when pertaining to a child is as follows:

Emotional abuse: *any type of abuse that involves the continual emotional mistreatment of a child. It's sometimes called psychological abuse and can involve deliberately trying to scare, humiliate, isolate or ignore a child* (NSPCC).

TYPES OF EMOTIONAL CHILD ABUSE

It can be hard to spot the signs of emotional child abuse, as it is often part of other kinds of abuse. However, it can also happen on its own. A child may not speak up right away or even realize that what they are enduring is emotional abuse. The following are all plausible examples:

- Being humiliated
- Being constantly criticized or joked about
- Being blamed constantly
- Being held up to impossible to achieve standards
- Not being allowed friendships
- Being manipulated (this will be further discussed in the coming sections)
- Not being recognized for success or congratulated
- Being ignored

- Not having your parents in your life
- Being exposed to unwanted behaviors, such as drug use
- Being called names, yelled at, and threatened

All of these types of emotional abuse are upsetting and greatly affect the social, mental, and emotional development of a child. You may recognize several of these, or only one or two. Regardless, even one of these types of abuse is enough to identify that you have been emotionally abused by your parents.

SIGNS OF EMOTIONAL CHILD ABUSE

As stated in the previous section, children do not always speak up when emotional abuse is occurring. This is for a variety of reasons. They might not realize that what is happening to them is unacceptable or they may fear for what will happen. They may be so badly abused that they have given up hope on finding help outside of their home. This is why many teachers, family members, and other safe adults should always be on the lookout for signs of potential emotional abuse. As children get older, their emotions begin to change. This can make it more difficult to recognize if abuse is occurring. For your own reference, try to think back on when you were younger and if any of the following signs ring true to your individual behavior:

- A lack of confidence and inability to reassure oneself
- Acting inappropriately for one's age
- Having difficulty making or maintaining friends
- Having difficulty controlling emotions and acting out

Often, it is assumed that the child who is being emotionally abused would not be attached to the caregiver or parent who is inflicting the abuse. However, this is not the case. Children are usually loyal to that parent because they are afraid of what will happen if they tell someone the true nature of what is happening. Also, they hope that if they behave well and act "right" as their abusive parent expects them to, they will once again receive that "sprinkle" of kindness we spoke about in the previous chapter. But this only allows for the abusive cycle to continue, as the child believes they are at fault and can fix it if they just do good enough.

THE ABUSE CYCLE

The emotional abuse cycle consists of four main parts: **Tension Building, Incident of Abuse, Reconciliation, and Calm.** This pattern of abusive behavior is what keeps victims trapped in the trauma bond with their abuser. Many people in romantic relationships also experience this cycle, as their abusive partner claims to never hurt them again but the cycle continues, worsening each time. The cycle was described in the 1970s by psychologist Lenore Walker in her book, *The Battered Woman.* In the book, she discussed evidence from interviews with women who had experienced abuse. Many professionals continue to use it today to describe the way abuse is perpetuated in all kinds of social relationships. The cycle varies slightly for each situation, although it proves as a useful model for most abuse victims. Let's take a look at each stage.

▷ Stage #1: Tension Building

We all know how stress can affect us negatively. We may feel agitated, be more easily upset, have higher emotional responses, etc. Anything can be a catalyst for tension. This includes work, trouble at home, illnesses, or fatigue. But if this tension builds up over time, more negative feelings soon follow, such as powerlessness and anger. As a child, you may have been able to sense when your parents were feeling stressed. Children are surprisingly perceptive and often know more than parents assume they do about what is going on. If you were able to sense this in your parents, you may have started "walking on eggshells" around them, doing all you could to avoid making them aim their anger at you. This can cause additional stress in children, as they feel on their guard and anxious and work overtime to meet the needs of their emotionally immature parents.

Example: John is in third grade, and his father picks him up from school every day. He makes sure to be at the pick-up point on time, as he knows that his father hates it when he is late. If he's late, his father will yell at him, then ignore him the rest of the night and sometimes the following day as well. When he gets in the car on Thursday afternoon, his father is on the phone talking to someone from work. He is upset, yelling at the person. This makes John anxious, and he quietly gets in the car and doesn't say anything. When they are halfway home, his father hangs up the phone. He asks John why he is so quiet and he says he was waiting for him to get off the phone.

▷ **Stage #2: Incident of Abuse**

Eventually, the abuser releases the tension. This is a way for them to gain control over their victim. In this stage, the incident of abuse involves any of the types discussed in the previous section. They may begin to blame the child for any of the problems or tension that they are feeling. *This is a conscious choice they make and although the tension can explain the abuse, it does **not** excuse it.* Abuse might involve any of the following:

- Insults/swearing
- Threats
- Controlling behavior
- Physical violence
- Emotional/mental manipulation

Example: After John explains to his father that he was only quiet because he was waiting for him to get off the phone, his father becomes angry and starts yelling at him. He says, "You are such an ungrateful child. I waste my time every day picking you up from school when I could be getting things done at work and you don't even say hello to me when you get in the car?" John feels his whole body tense up and even though he is used to his father flying off the handle, he still feels fear when he gets angry like this. He tries to calm him down by saying, "I'm sorry, Dad, I didn't want to interrupt your phone call." His father shakes his head and ignores him for the rest of the night.

▷ **Stage #3: Reconciliation**

After the abuse takes place, the tension will fade. This happens naturally, as we all have stressors in our life that come and go. However, the abuser then will try and move past the abuse as if it never took place. They may try to reconcile with the victim by giving gifts, saying kind words, or performing other acts that completely contradict the behavior that they displayed during the abuse incident. It is in this stage that dopamine is released. As we explained in the previous chapter, this is connected to the pleasure center of our brain and it makes us further bond with the abuser. In this stage, children often think they have their "real" parents back.

Example: When John's father picks him up the next day at school, he is not on the phone, and he is the first to say hello. He is waiting outside the car for him and says, "Hi, buddy!" as he sees him coming out of the school. This makes John feel good and especially relieved since his father is no longer ignoring him. His father gives him a big hug before he opens the door for John to get in the car. "How about some ice cream?" he asks. John feels great, and the two of them go for ice cream.

▷ **Stage #4: Calm**

In between instances of abuse, there is usually calm. Things cannot always be crazy or others might notice. Your parents may have even made excuses or justified the abuse during this stage by apologizing or blaming others for their behavior, minimizing the abuse, or accusing you of provoking them when you "knew they were stressed." They might show that they are sorry and promise you it will never happen again. This makes you wonder, *maybe it was my fault, and it wasn't all that bad.* But this is a form of gaslighting, which will be defined in the next section. This calm gives children some relief from the pain of abuse but it also gives them a false sense of security that it won't happen again.

Example: On the weekend that follows, John and his parents have a relaxing time. They go to the park, they go out to dinner Saturday night, and everything seems normal again. His father even tells John that he "wasn't himself last week" because his boss was stressing him out. He says that this week will be much less stressful at work. John feels relieved and stops worrying that his dad will get angry at him for a bit. However, the following week, he overhears a late-night argument between his father and mother and the next day, he worries all day at school about when his father will pick him up.

▷ **Cycle Recap**

This cycle continues to repeat. The length of time between each stage and cycle can vary. As the abuse escalates, the lulls will shorten. It can get to the point where the calm stage completely disappears. In this example, the abuse for John often happens when he is picked up from school by his father. But abuse does not have to happen the same way every time. Emotional and mental abuse is often overlooked and can be tricky to identify. This is why next we will discuss some specific manipulation tactics that your parents may have used on you as a child. This can be particularly illuminating to read as an adult because it can explain certain confusing emotions you had as a child.

Keep in mind that anyone can be a victim of abuse. There is no "typical victim." While we are centering on the parent-child relationship, this abuse cycle is relevant for all kinds of abusive dynamics. Victims of abuse can be from any age group, background, education or economic level, ethnicities, and lifestyle. Additionally, anyone can be a perpetrator of abuse. Abusing others is a learned behavior. Those who witness it growing up, like children, may believe that it is normal and then go on to inflict it on others. This is why it is so important to recognize how wrong it is and break the cycle from happening with other people in your life, and especially with your own children. We want to prevent you from becoming both a perpetrator of the abuse cycle and ever being a victim again. When abusive behavior feels normal, it can be easier to enter other unhealthy relationships, as the dynamics feel regular and habitual.

In John's case, he is being **emotionally and mentally abused** by his father. In Stage #2, we see his father yell at him for not saying hello to him, even though he was on the phone. He does this to shame him and blame him for "doing something wrong," even though he didn't do anything wrong at all. This is a way for him to boost his own ego by putting his son down. There are all sorts of psychological terms for what occurred in this example and we are going to discuss them in the following section. Putting a label on the abuse you may have endured will help you better understand and empathize with what you went through and it will help you be able to better identify it in the future.

PSYCHOLOGICAL MANIPULATION TACTICS

Psychologically manipulating someone is a cruel form of abuse. When it is done to a child, it is especially awful because a child cannot fight back or stand up for themselves. When someone is being manipulated, they are going through a distortion of their own thoughts and emotions. The person inflicting the abuse is looking to gain control over them in an attempt to get what they want. There are many different forms that manipulation can take but we are going to cover some of the most common tactics used by emotionally immature parents. As we go through them, try to identify the ones you may have gone through yourself growing up.

▷ **Tactic #1: Gaslighting**

Gaslighting is when an abuser makes their victim question their judgments and reality. The victim then begins to wonder if they are going crazy or losing their sanity (Gordon, 2021). Abusive people use this to exert power and to get what they want from others. If this has happened to you, you may have started to question your own perception of reality. Leaving a conversation with a gaslighter makes you feel confused and wondering if something might be wrong with you. This is particularly damaging for children because they are still growing and cultivating their sense of themselves and reality. Some characteristics and phrases of gaslighters include the following:

- **Lying:** Gaslighters lie consistently. This is how they skew your reality and change stories.
  Even if you know they are not telling the truth, they can be convincing. It can be shocking how blatantly they will lie. Even if both of you just witnessed something, they may completely change the narrative of the reality of the situation in an attempt to make you question everything, even if just for a second. Manipulation happens over time, slowly chipping away at your sanity. Common phrases include, *"You are making that up!"* and

"That (event/situation/conversation) never happened."

- **Discrediting**: Abusive parents are known to talk bad about their children to other people. This is in an attempt to discredit anything they might say. This is also done so as to cover themselves in case their child decides to actually speak up about some of the abuse occurring at home. You might even overhear this at family functions or in school. This is hurtful for the child, not only because they hear their own parents talking negatively about them, but because the things they say are untrue! This further discourages them from speaking up and asking for help when emotional abuse is taking place. Common phrases include, *"Katy is a sweet kid, but she has a terrible memory!"* and *"Matt is always lying. I think I should take him to see someone."*

- **Minimizing**: To a gaslighter, your emotions do not exist or they are an overreaction. This is to communicate to you that what you are feeling is wrong or "too dramatic." When you are in an environment where someone constantly tells you that your thoughts and feelings are not valid, you will naturally begin to question yourself. This can be damaging to children, as they are learning to be their own individual and this will make them unable to trust their intuition. Instead, it will make them dependent upon their abusive parent. This can even create a **codependent** dynamic, one that will be explored in later chapters. Instead of becoming their own individual person, they will rely on reacting to the feelings of their parent. When your parents minimize any of your feelings, they shut down your ability to express yourself. This has long-term effects, as it does not give you the chance for emotional development. Common phrases your parents may use are *"You are too sensitive."* or *"Would you calm down? You always overreact!"*

- **Blame Shifting**: Every time you discuss something with your parents, somehow you end up being blamed at the end. Maybe you tried to tell them how they hurt your feelings or upset you and they twisted the conversation so much that, in the end, you were the one apologizing! They make you feel that if only you had behaved differently, then all of this could have been avoided. Parents often blame the child for their mistakes. They do not take responsibility and instead will make the child feel that everything is somehow their fault. If they were to take responsibility, that would mean they would have to confront reality and this would contradict the point of their manipulation! Common phrases include: *"If you didn't make me so mad, I wouldn't have screamed at you like that!"* or *"It's all your fault that we can't do (blank) because you never stop distracting me."*

* This is what we saw in our earlier example with John. His father blames John for his temper by saying that if only he didn't have to pick him up every day, he could get things done at work. Of course, this isn't John's fault, but through repeated gaslighting, John will begin to question his reality and take on blame that does not belong to him.

- **Compassion as a Weapon**: Your parents may have used kind words to try to minimize or calm a tense situation. This often happens during **Stage #4: Calm**. They are the words you wanted to hear, but they do not have any real truth behind them. This also usually happens when they are trying to get you to tell them something which they will later use against you. Common phrases include: *"I love you so much, and I would never do anything to hurt you."* or *"You're my child! I will always protect you."*

▷ Tactic #2: Projection

This tactic happens when the abuser displaces their feelings onto another person, animal, or object (Psychology Today, n.d.). In this case, your parents were placing their feelings onto you. Most commonly, it is in defense of their own unacceptable behavior. Similar to blame shifting, it is when the parent knows that a feeling or behavior of theirs is wrong and they do not want to accept responsibility for it. Let's look at an example:

Example: Nicole has gymnastics practice at 3 o'clock on Saturday. She reminds her mother because sometimes she forgets. On Saturdays, Nicole usually does her homework, then watches her younger siblings while her mother sleeps. She is in eighth grade and the oldest of her four siblings. Her mother works 40 hours a week and expects Nicole to watch them while she sleeps on Saturday. Around 2 o'clock, Nicole gets dressed and packs her bag for gymnastics. She also tries to wake up her mother, but she just rolls over. She waits until 2:30 p.m., then goes back in and wakes her again. Her mother sees the time and gets angry. "Why didn't you wake me earlier?" she snaps. Nicole assures her that she tried to. Her mother jumps out of bed and they rush to gymnastics. They get there 15 minutes late and before she goes inside, Nicole's mother yells at her, calling her lazy and "useless."

She says, "If you were responsible enough to get me up in time, we would have been here at 3 o'clock."

In this example, Nicole did nothing wrong. In contrast, she is actually doing much more than a child her age should be doing. She is caring for several other young children while her mother sleeps the entire day, she is getting herself ready for gymnastics, and is acting as an adult's alarm clock. Yet, her mother does not get up when she should and blames Nicole for it.

▷ **Tactic #3: Scapegoat**

In a family where there are emotionally immature parents, particularly **narcissistic parents,** there is often a family *"scapegoat child."* This is the child who is blamed for everything. All the negative attention is deflected onto them so the family does not have to address the real, internal conflict that is the abuse. The term scapegoat comes from the Hebrew tradition of the annual Day of Atonement where a goat was cursed with the sins of the nation and wandered and died in the wilderness as a sacrifice (Grande, 2021). Therefore, the scapegoat child is blamed for everything, burdened with the "sins" or wrongdoings of the adults in the family.

"SPLITTING:" AT THE CORE OF
PSYCHOLOGICAL MANIPULATION

Many children cannot recognize, let alone comprehend why they are feeling confused, blamed, or not valued. These and so much more are some of the effects of psychological abuse. We will discuss just how this abuse may have affected you and may continue to affect you in Chapter Five. But for now, you may be wondering, *How can someone inflict abuse one day, then act like all is fine the next?* This is because those who inflict abuse are emotionally immature or suffer from narcissistic personality disorder also often experience the psychological phenomenon known as ***splitting***.

Splitting: *Also known as black and white thinking; when someone views aspects of their lives in a false dichotomy in which everything is either good or bad* (Drake, 2021).

Splitters are either in favor of a person or against them at any given time. Life, in general, is divided into two parts. Think of your parents and their general behavior. *How did they view the world? What about their job? How did they react to conflicts with other people in your family? When they interacted with you, was it either good or terrible?* We all split to a certain degree throughout our life. It can be difficult to view certain areas of our life as "grey." However, those who divide people into categories without taking into account their feelings can be abusive.

Many of these "splitters" often use this to justify their actions. You may have made a mistake as a child or they may have perceived that to be so and they used this to justify their abuse. Recognize now that this is not acceptable behavior, especially for a parent who is supposed to be a loving guide for a growing child. Hopefully, the cycle discussed in this chapter helped to highlight and explain some of the confusing or harmful experiences you had as a child. The manipulation tactics are often less known, but once brought to light, they can affirm that you are not crazy or imagining things. The emotional abuse you endured was not a product of your actions or behavior.

TRAUMA & THE MEMORY

This chapter can be overwhelming! As you are reading, you may find that certain things "click" for you and you may begin to put together missing pieces of your childhood. You may be wondering, *Why is it hard for me to remember certain years or events from my abusive childhood?* This is because traumatic events can actually affect our memory. Certain details may endure but others, known as peripheral details, are not retained quite as well (Sawchuk, 2018). Our memory process involves three stages:

1. **Encoding**: adding information
2. **Storage**: retaining information
3. **Retrieval**: assessing/recalling the information

The traumatizing event typically becomes encoded in the memory and stored so it can later be recalled. Some people struggle with ruminations or flashbacks of the event as well. But the peripheral details, such as the time of year, place, etc. are not usually as well encoded, so they are not stored and cannot be recalled. *Essentially, the traumatic event becomes the center of the memory, making it the most memorable and easily encoded* (Sawchuk, 2018).This pushes the other details aside, making that information more difficult to remember years later.

So, if you find that you have trouble remembering exactly how old you were or where you were when certain abusive situations took place, do not allow yourself to become upset about this. Many abuse victims do this, and they even start to second guess themselves, wondering: *Did that actually happen? Maybe I am crazy.* This only gives in to the manipulation you endured and discredits your experience. Be kind to yourself and know that what happened was real. I

believe you, but more importantly, you believe in yourself. And that is what matters the most.

CHAPTER SUMMARY

- Emotional abuse is any type of abuse that
  involves the continual emotional mistreatment
  of a child. Children are usually loyal to the
  abusive parent because they are afraid of what
  will happen if they tell someone the true nature
  of what is happening. Also, they hope that if
  they behave well and act "right," as their abusive
  parent expects them to, then they will once
  again receive that "sprinkle" of kindness.
- The emotional abuse cycle consists of four
  main parts: **tension building, incident of
  abuse, reconciliation, and calm.**
- Emotionally immature parents use several
  abusive psychological manipulation tactics such
  as gaslighting, projection, and scapegoating.

In the next chapter, you will learn what to do now that
you are a parent and how the way you raise your children will reflect forever in your life and theirs.

4

NOW THAT I AM A PARENT...

The dictionary definition could not begin to define the meaning of being a *parent* for any of us. In the dictionary, we only have the scientific version. However, this is not exactly what we will be talking about in this chapter. We want to discuss what it truly means to be a parent, how much we have to sacrifice ourselves, and what it's like to truly put the needs of another human being before our own. I did find a great definition of motherhood that I particularly connected with.

Motherhood: *It's exhausting, inspiring, soul-sucking, and purpose-giving. It makes you question everything, while also feeling like you know it all* (Joyce, 2019).

Everything about this definition feels right. Being a parent tires you out! It takes everything from you. But at the same time, it inspires you to be the best you can be for your children and it gives you a purpose and drive like no other. Ask yourself, *How do I define motherhood or fatherhood? What does it mean to me to be a parent?* Only you know what it means to you. We all have different versions and different ideas of what is most important when it comes to parenting our children. However, to me, being a parent is the most important job in the world. The way we raise our children and the way our parents raised us will reflect forever in our lives. The actions of parental figures will shape the lives of the children in their care for the bad or the good, all depending on their actions. Ask yourself another question, *How are you shaping the lives of your children?*

Taking responsibility for the lives of our children is exhausting. The definition above hit that nail on the head! When we grew up in an environment without positive role models, we must take matters into our own hands. It is our job to provide a safe, stable, and caring environment for our kids. *Why is it that so many people believe being a parent does not require any prior awareness or research?* If we want to ensure not to repeat the same patterns as our parents, we must make a conscious effort every day. It can be exhausting and it is going to be hard work. You have already started the work since you are reading this book and the payoff will make it all worth it.

THE LEGAL RESPONSIBILITIES OF BEING A PARENT

No matter how you view and define parenthood, there are *legal* responsibilities that all parents must take on when caring for their child. However, only adhering to these aspects alone will not make you a great parent. You are morally responsible for your child. This and the following things are non-negotiable when it comes to your role in raising your child. You are legally obligated to all of the following:

- *Giving the child a home*
- *Disciplining the child*
- *Protecting and maintaining the child*
- *Being responsible for primary and secondary education*
- *Handling the child's medical needs*
- *Naming the child*
- *Protecting & maintaining the child's property*

You may read this list and feel that your parents did not complete one or several of these for you. This is typical of emotionally immature parents, especially when there is abuse present in the home. "Protecting and maintaining the child" does not refer to only caring for physical needs, but also mental and emotional needs. Therefore, when your parents did not care for your feelings and mental well-being, they were not meeting their legal duties as responsible parents.

BEING A GREAT PARENT

The previous section outlines what is required of a parent legally. Only ensuring these aspects will not make you a great parent and will not help you strongly connect to your child. Being a great parent is about understanding, patience, and openness. Your parents may have approached their parenting duties as if they were a job. But there is so much joy and love in taking care of your own child! Recognition and appreciation are what sets apart a great parent from others. Some examples of a great parent include all of the following traits:

- *Patience when the child is being difficult*
- *Respect for the beliefs of the child*
- *Consistency*
- *Adapting to stressful situations*
- *Willing to talk to the child about problems or uncomfortable topics*

- *Approaching the child from a place of love*
- *Knowing when to take time for themselves to ensure they are at their best to care for the child*

TYPICAL PARENTING STYLES

People everywhere raise their children differently. You may have friends who are extremely strict with their children and others who have no curfew for their teenagers. Often, these opposites do not approve of each other. But there is no right or wrong answer, as your method will be unique to you. *However, our parenting style can be affected by how we were raised.* This is critical to be aware of because an abusive environment is not acceptable for our children and it is not something we wish to repeat! You can make the conscious choice to raise your children differently than you were raised. While each of our styles is unique, as mentioned, many times there is an overall category that our style can fit into as well. There are five common parenting styles, and we will discuss the advantages and disadvantages of each one below.

1. **Balanced**: This style is exactly as it sounds, balanced! Usually, your parenting hangs somewhere in between independence and being together as a family. You are not overly strict

but you do not let your kids behave in whatever manner they choose either. In balanced parenting, you support your child's wellbeing but are not overprotective to the point where your child cannot make mistakes. These mistakes are crucial for them to learn and grow. In a balanced parenting style, there are often set rules; however, these rules are not unreasonable. They are in place to help the children stay safe, learn how to function in a socially acceptable way, and become strong-functioning adults.

2. **Neutral**: In this style, the child will have a high level of independence. Sadly, there is less of a connection between the parent and the child. The parent may have low emotional responsiveness, and therefore, the rules are not regularly enforced. The child has a great deal of free time to make mistakes and their developmental life may suffer because of it. The parent quite literally takes a neutral approach to raising the child. They let things happen, allowing the child to have a great deal of experience in handling situations on their own. This can be good for the child's maturity; however, they may be exposed to things too early.

3. **Nonrestrictive**: Similar to the neutral style, this parenting style does not enforce rules. However, the parent and child usually have a close connection. This is a good thing, but it tends to prevent the parent from "being in charge." The parent will always compromise to keep the child happy at all times. This parenting style is more of a friendship than a parent-child relationship. If the child gets upset because a rule is being enforced, the parent will cave in and let them do what they want. This teaches them a negative lesson, namely that if they just complain or ask for something long enough, then they will get what they want.

4. **Strict**: This is another style with a lower level of emotional closeness, but also with a low level of flexibility. There are strict rules which should not be broken. If they are broken, there are swift and harsh consequences. Children raised in this style tend to be obedient and highly focused. However, their creativity and ability to make their own mistakes are limited. They do not have the same opportunity as other children to have experiences and learn from them. Instead, they often continue to enforce strict rules for themselves going into adulthood.

5. **Overbearing**: The parent and child are close emotionally in this style. The parent is also very protective. There is a strict set of rules with consequences if they are broken, much like the strict style. However, the child can also sense their parent's fears. They often become anxious, afraid of all of the same things that their parents are afraid of, and overprotective. They may develop phobias or have other mental illnesses such as generalized anxiety disorder.

There is nothing inherently wrong with any of these parenting styles. Your version may be a variation of one of these or something completely different! What you don't want to engage in is manipulation, emotional abuse, or role reversal, in which your child must take on the responsibilities of a parent. The child should never be blamed for the parent's shortcomings, as you often were by your parents. As illustrated by these common parenting styles, none of us are perfect! *Parents are just human beings who are doing their best to raise other good humans.* If you are reading this book, then you are already putting in more effort and compassion than your parents did. In Chapter Six, we will look at specific examples and strategies for you to break the cycle and ensure that your style of parenting does not replicate that of your own parents.

FREUD'S PERSPECTIVE

Sigmund Freud (1856-1939) was the founder of *psycho-analysis*. This type of therapy is a way of treating mental illness that works to explain human behavior by investigating the conscious and unconscious mind by uncovering repressed fears that often trace back to childhood (McLeod, 2018). Many times we will see this type of therapy in movies, with one of the characters laying on a couch telling stories of their childhood to a therapist sitting across from them in a chair, holding a notebook. Freud argued that parents play a defining role in how children's personalities form. Not only this, but they also affect the formation of their emotional and mental health. Before him, many people thought parents only taught their children manners and how to be polite, such as the appropriate time to say "please" or "thank you."

Freud additionally stated that parents can influence a child's unconscious mind and be a large factor in how they view themselves and the world around them. Therefore, much of your child's behavior cannot simply be explained by how they consciously think or feel. Let's look at the difference between our *conscious* and *unconscious* minds, according to Freud.

The conscious mind: *all of our thoughts, memories, feelings, and wishes that we are aware of; our rational thought processes; includes our memory which can be brought into awareness* (Cherry, 2020).

The unconscious mind: *feelings, thoughts, urges, memories outside of our awareness; may be unacceptable/unpleasant; feelings of anxiety or pain* (Cherry, 2020).

With the power to influence the unconscious mind of our children, we must not only be aware of this but be gentle and think before we act. The unconscious mind will influence our children for the rest of their lives. Consider yourself now and just how your own unconscious mind may still continue to affect you because of events that happened during your childhood. *Would you want your own children to deal with this same pain?*

START BREAKING THE TOXIC CYCLE

So, how do we gauge our parenting skills? It can be difficult to do so simply by watching the behavior of our children. There will be great days when our kids love us, behave perfectly, and everything is great! Then, there will be days when your world feels as if it is in absolute chaos. And this is normal for all families! This is the messy nature of raising tiny humans. Recognizing that what you learn as a child has a lasting impact on you will set you up for success. Being raised by your emotionally immature parents helped you to understand how the negative messages you learn can stick with you.

Something you can do is decide to spare your children from suffering from negative childhood messages that will haunt them into their adulthood. Instead of being another generation of toxic parents, take this as an opportunity to rise above it and parent in a healthier, more loving, and considerate way. Keep in mind: we have two options for dealing with our past. *We can either repeat what happened to us or we can work hard and strive for better.* What's important is your commitment to breaking the cycle. Make the choice now to not repeat the same patterns as your parents did. In Chapter Six, we will go through a detailed plan on how you can stop the cycle and parent in a way that is healthy, supportive, and beneficial for the relationship between you and your children.

CHAPTER SUMMARY

- Being a parent tires you out, inspires you to be the best you can be for the children, and gives you a purpose and drive like no other. What it means to be a parent differs for all of us, but only you can decide what it means for you.

- Sigmund Freud stated that parents can influence a child's unconscious mind and be a large factor in how they view themselves and the world around them as adults.
- We have two options for dealing with our past: *We can either repeat what happened to us or we can work hard and strive for better.*

In the next chapter, you will learn the effects toxic parents have on the lives of their children.

5

TOXIC PARENTS ARE RUINING THEIR CHILDREN'S LIVES WITHOUT NOTICING IT

I n Chapter Three we spoke about *child emotional abuse*, its different types, and potential signs. With emotionally immature parents, you suffered this and endured the abuse cycle, manipulation tactics, and more at the hands of those who were supposed to care for you and protect you. It's crucial to recognize just how damaging this can be. The effects carry on into adulthood and as you read this book, hopefully, you are recognizing instances from your childhood and are finally able to put a name to situations that you knew were wrong. To further validate your feelings toward the abuse you endured throughout your childhood, let's take a look at the differences between a healthy and a dysfunctional family dynamic.

HEALTHY VS. DYSFUNCTIONAL FAMILY DYNAMICS

It's important to note that all families will be dysfunctional at some point because we are all humans and no one is perfect! If you find a lot of factors from the right column apply to your family situation, they need to change. Unless they do, they will negatively impact the child and have lasting effects.

Healthy	Dysfunctional
• Accepts emotional expressions	• Lack of empathy & respect
• Consistent rules & boundaries	• No respect for boundaries; invasion of privacy
• Feelings of safety & security	• Extreme conflicts & feelings of hostility
• Parents provide care	• Conditional love; emotional, verbal, or physical abuse
• Responsibilities are age-appropriate	• Role-reversal; children take on parental responsibility
• Forgiving of mistakes	• Unrealistic expectations

Children who grow up in a dysfunctional family environment are the *innocent* ones. It is likely that your parents tried to make you feel that everything was somehow your fault, when, of course, it could not have been! As a child, you had no control over the toxic environment that you were exposed to. The repeated abuse and trauma cause scarring that absolutely alters the growth and nurturing of an ***individual self.***

Self: *the totality of the individual, consisting of all characteristic attributes, conscious and unconscious, mental and physical* (The American Psychological Association, n.d.).

Instead of having the normal time to foster this sense of self in childhood that we all should have, you may have instead taken on various parenting roles and responsibilities that your emotionally immature parents could not or would not do themselves. This meant you missed out on vital aspects of your childhood experience and growth. In an attempt to escape these painful experiences from your past, you may have engaged in destructive behaviors. These can include substance abuse, negative inner feelings, and repeating the abuse you once endured. *Healthy families return to normal functioning after a particular situation or crisis ends. However, in a dysfunctional family, the problems seem to never go away and they are a strong undercurrent of the family dynamic.*

DYSFUNCTIONAL HOUSEHOLD TYPES

Just as there are different types of emotionally immature parents, there are also different types of dysfunctional households. It's important to recognize that these households are created by emotionally immature parents and you may notice similarities between the household and the parent types.

- **Chronic Conflict**: In this household, there is always an issue! Perhaps the parents are always fighting with one another, causing constant stress and negative feelings in the house. This is the most common dynamic within dysfunctional households, as the parents have a turbulent relationship which is witnessed by the children. One parent may always be coming and going or have a problem with their anger. However, it does not always have to be a conflict between the parents. In some dysfunctional dynamics, there is constant conflict between the parents and children. This leads to high stress levels and a constant feeling of never knowing what to expect.

- **Pathological**: In this house, there are mental health issues or substance abuse issues. One or both of the emotionally immature parents are suffering from these pathological problems, causing the children to take on the role of being the caretakers in order to keep the household going. Because emotionally immature parents always place themselves in the victim position, a pathological issue will only further this. Children with sick, emotionally immature parents, whether that be a physical or mental illness, learn how to take care of other people instead of themselves. Children are innocent and should be cared for! This is a seriously damaging type of dysfunctional household because the child is not allowed to act or feel like one.

- **Chaotic**: Regardless of which type of parent you connected your parents to from Chapter One, most households with immature parents are chaotic. The children are not looked after properly, the parents are busy with other things or just not present. There are no rules or expectations, and most of all, *no consistency.* Also similar to the **chronic conflict** household, the chaotic household may have parents who are coming and going. Maybe they are in other relationships, have multiple jobs, or just lack overall stability.

- **Dominant-submissive**: In this house, there is one dictator parent who is in charge and calls all the shots. This happens often when there is a *narcissistic parent*, as they need things to be their way all the time. However, the other parent is usually depressed, unhappy, and projecting these emotions onto the children. This is also a terrible illustration of how a romantic relationship should be for the children. They view the relationship as normal and may go on to repeat these patterns in their own romantic relationships in the future.

- **Emotionally Distant**: Certain families do not show love or affection, depending on their unique social or cultural background. But children should feel comfortable opening up to their parents, showing their emotions, and knowing they are in a safe environment to do so. This might be the least obvious dysfunctional type, as it is not always overt to other people. But it can be damaging when children do not feel safe expressing their inner life to their parents. They are also learning a negative lesson on how to communicate with those they are close to.

Living with emotionally immature parents can include traits from all of these household types. It is possible that your parents were suffering from pathological problems, had a negative romantic relationship, always had problems, and were emotionally distant from each other and their children. *Phew!* While this chapter is overwhelming, it's important to discuss the difficult stuff. Fully understanding just how this kind of childhood affects a person's development and life into adulthood will bring awareness to the importance of ending the cycle and working toward a parenting style that is healthy for both you and your children.

SIX ROLES OF CHILDREN IN DYSFUNCTIONAL FAMILIES

Because children are resilient, they learn quickly how to adapt and survive in this chaotic environment. But this often means they must take on roles that no longer support their own growth and experience as a child. They instead perform the duties their parents should be doing, learn hard life lessons too early, become rebellious, and more. There are several basic roles children commonly fall into when trying to cope with a dysfunctional family dynamic:

1. **The Peacekeeper**: This child works to diffuse the chaotic energy in the house. Whenever tension rises between their parents or between their parents and siblings, this child mediates and reduces tension. This could be out of a level of maturity learned early due to their situation or feelings of anxiety and a desperate attempt to keep their family together. Regardless, they are constantly on alert, taking on the role of a mature parent in order to keep things as calm as possible. Living in a chronic conflict

household is an exhausting way of life for the peacekeeper. They cannot focus on themselves or their childhood, as they are always waiting for the next problem to arise, all the while knowing that they will be the only one to take care of it.

2. **The Rebel**: This child is rebellious. They are always getting into trouble at school, acting out, and causing problems within this family. In this way, they are distracting the parents from themselves! This too can be conscious or unconscious. But they use their rebellious actions as a way to let out the pent-up energy of the negative household environment they are enduring. Doing so is also a way they try to consciously or unconsciously let other people know something is wrong.

3. **The Scapegoat**: In Chapter Three, we discussed the role of the *scapegoat child*. This family member takes the blame for everything and finds all the negative attention in the household directed at them. The parents will use them as the reason for why things are dysfunctional in the household instead of taking responsibility. This child usually has low self-esteem, feeling like no matter what they do or say in the house, they just can't seem to get anything right.

4. **The Lost Child**: This is the quiet one. They are usually ignored as they try to disappear out of fear of upsetting the parents and becoming the next target. They are lost because without a sense of security or direction from their parents, they feel intense anxiety and fear surrounding their home life at all times. This extends into their life in school and socially, as they learn that staying quiet may keep them safer than speaking up for what they truly need and want.

5. **The Charmer**: This may also be called the "favorite." This child is clever and uses comedy to distract from the real issues happening in the house. The parents often favor this child as they are a good distraction. The charmer makes jokes or makes light of situations, and they are similar to the peacekeeper in the sense that they also work to diffuse the chronic conflicts that arise in the household. This is also exhausting for the charmer because even though they may appear happy and comical on the outside, their inner life is often riddled with unhappiness and insecurity.

6. **The Mastermind**: Also a manipulator, this child has taken a hint from their parents! They know how to capitalize on the mistakes and

faults of their parents and siblings. They will use this to get whatever they want. They also might create issues between family members when they know tensions are already high in order to place themselves higher up in the eyes of the emotionally immature parent. This, too, is just a way for them to try and survive in the unstable environment created by the adults.

While it is interesting how different children adapt to various roles, it is also extremely sad. No child should have to morph their personality into something completely different in order to survive in a home with parents who should be caring for them. But sadly, this is only the start. These roles are only how the children react while still living with their parents. The effects of the abuse in these kinds of dysfunctional homes are more damaging in the long term.

THE THREE AREAS AFFECTED BY EMOTIONAL ABUSE

Over time, emotional abuse will have effects on a child. This often happens in three ways, **behavioral, emotional, and mental**. These three aspects are the most affected because a child does not understand how to process the abuse they are enduring and their mind and body go into a kind of overdrive attempting to handle it.

- **Behavioral Problems**: A child's behavior changes throughout their growth. But when there is emotional abuse, it can alter this natural progression. Those in abusive situations may want attention or become clingy to the abusive parent. This is in an attempt to keep them happy and try to act how they "should." But this can quickly create problems in school and in their social life, as they will have a harder time forming outside relationships. On the other hand, some children stop caring about how they act or what happens to them. This is often because no matter how they behave, their parents end up yelling or abusing them anyway! *This makes them feel out of control* and their behavior reflects this feeling. Some children appear as if they are actively trying to make others dislike them, by being offensive or engaging in risky behavior, such as stealing or bullying.
- **Emotional Development**: Because parents are supposed to create an environment where children feel safe expressing their emotions, children are able to develop proper emotions

and learn how and when to express them. But when there is no stable, healthy environment for them to do so, children may have difficulty controlling their emotions or expressing them appropriately. This can create a lack of confidence and difficulty with maintaining relationships, as others will see them as impulsive or angry. A stunted emotional development can lead to higher levels of depression and other health problems.

- **Mental Health Problems**: This can include *depression, anxiety, or suicidal thoughts.* Some children have been known to develop eating disorders as a way to try to keep some control over themselves. Others self-harm. These mental health problems are a result of the brain's reaction to emotional abuse, which will be discussed more in depth in the next section.

SO, HOW DOES THIS HAPPEN?

These effects are detrimental long after childhood, *but how exactly does emotional abuse cause these consequences in children?* As children grow and develop, their brains undergo periods of **rapid development** or critical periods of growth within the brain. When they have negative experiences, these periods can be disrupted.

This alters brain chemistry later in life. This means that the timing and duration of the emotional abuse greatly impact how negative the outcomes will be.

Researchers at McLean Hospital, Harvard Medical School, and Northeastern University all studied the connection between abuse and brain structure. They used MRI technology to identify changes in the structure of brain chemistry in young adults with a history of childhood abuse or neglect. There were clear differences found between those who experienced abuse and those who did not. The regions affected were *those that balanced emotions, impulses, and self-awareness*. They also concluded that people with a history of abuse had an increased risk of developing mental health issues (Holmes, 2021).

EFFECTS ON BRAIN STRUCTURE

When the abuse happens during times of rapid development in childhood, there are many important areas of the brain affected (Holmes, 2021). These areas are often responsible for our emotions, memory, and perception. Let's take a look at a few specific ways the brain will develop differently:

1. Decreased Size

- **Corpus Callosum**: responsible for motor, sensory, and cognitive performance
- **Hippocampus**: learning and memory

2. Lower volume

- **Prefrontal Cortex**: behavior, emotional balance, and perception
- **Cerebellum**: motor skills and coordination

3. Dysfunction

- **Hypothalamic-pituitary-adrenal axis**: stress response

4. Overactivity

- **Amygdala**: emotion regulation and risk assessment

CONSEQUENCES OF THE AFFECTED BRAIN STRUCTURE

Because these regions of the brain are so critical for our behavior, emotions, and social function, there are many consequences when they are not functioning properly. These will continue to cause issues in adulthood if they are not addressed. You may have noticed or still notice the additional following symptoms:

- Feeling constantly on alert
- Inability to relax
- Feeling afraid most of the time
- Learning deficits
- Difficulty functioning in typical social situations
- Developing mental health conditions
- Inability to process positive feedback

As an adult, you may find relationships are difficult, whether they are personal or professional. It is harder for children of abuse to relate to others after forming **unhealthy attachments** to their parents. This is due to something called the *attachment theory*.

Attachment Theory: *This argues that primary caregivers who are available and responsive to an infant's needs allow the child to develop a sense of security. The infant knows the caregiver is dependable, and this creates a secure base for them to explore the rest of the world* (Cherry, 2019).

Research shows that children who fail to form secure attachment early in life will have negative consequences later in their childhood and in their adulthood. There are four patterns of attachment for children: **ambivalent, avoidant, disorganized, and secure**. Secure is the kind of attachment parents should strive for, as it occurs when children feel reassured and safe no matter what the situation is or regardless of what kind of negative emotions they may be having at the time. However, the other types occur in a dysfunctional household in which the parents are emotionally immature and there may be emotional or mental abuse occurring.

- **Ambivalent**: In this style, children are distressed when a parent leaves and the parents are typically absent, creating a desperate need for the children to want to be around them. This is a *fragile* attachment style because love may be given quickly then suddenly taken away. Similarly, the parent may be present for a stretch of time and then gone.

Example: Ben is seven years old and going to his grandmother's house for the weekend. He goes there often because his father works a lot and his mother is always busy. But when she drops him off, he typically has a breakdown, crying and begging for her to stay. It takes him several hours to calm down. He is reassured that she will pick him up on Sunday, but when Sunday comes, she often doesn't come back to get him until Monday or Tuesday.

- **Avoidant**: Children avoid their parents as the parents are typically abusive or neglectful, creating fear in their own children. This happens when the parents do not provide necessities for their children such as food, shelter, or emotional availability. The child will also then avoid or disregard their own needs in order to try and keep their parents close.

Example: Andrea's father has a temper. She loves school and is at the top of her eighth-grade class. She just received a 99% on her science test and is feeling good about it. She is excited to tell her father because she knows how important it is to him that she does good in school. But as she gets home in the afternoon, Andrea finds out that he has been drinking all day and he is arguing with and screaming at her mother. She quietly goes right to her room in order to avoid upsetting him further.

- **Disorganized**: Children are confused and disoriented and may resist the parent because the parenting is inconsistent, creating confusion in how the child should behave. They know that the parent is not a secure source of safety and emotional reassurance; therefore, they have trouble reacting to emotional closeness.

Example: Michael's father is rarely home. He comes home about once a month and the rest of the time he is away. Michael asks his mother where he goes but she never gives him a solid answer. He is only four, so he doesn't understand. Eventually, each time his father does come home after being away, he runs behind his mother and won't give him a hug or speak to him at all.

Once these unhealthy attachments are formed, they have a way of carrying into adulthood. They are learned behaviors and may continue to be repeated unless properly addressed. There are many varieties that can affect the attachment theory that is formed, such as how old the child was when the abuse occurred, how long it continued, or if there were any interventions.

CONDITIONAL VS. UNCONDITIONAL LOVE

The difference between conditional and unconditional love is important for children of abuse to understand because though they may have heard the phrase, "I love you," this often came along with conditions and was never a statement that left them feeling secure and comforted. Let's look at the difference between the two.

Conditional Love: *love with conditions; love for another person is contingent on certain actions* (Hudson Therapy).

When we talk about conditional love, there are often plenty of "ifs" attached. *Did you hear this word throughout your childhood?* Your parents may have said, "I will love you if you do (blank)," or "I won't get angry if you do exactly as I say," or "I won't ignore you if (blank)." These are all examples of conditional love *because you were expected to act a certain way in order to receive their affection.* Conditional love causes children to feel a lack of stability and trust. They know they have to act and be a certain way in order to continue receiving the love they desperately need. This is damaging to their attachment style, and it teaches them that they must change who they are in order to be cherished, appreciated, and loved.

Unconditional Love: *love without conditions; no matter what someone does, they will always be loved* (Hudson Therapy).

This is true love. However, it isn't easy! As a parent, there are times when your children may be extremely difficult or frustrating and you may be tempted to say things that are not too kind. But love takes effort and patience, and your children deserve it. You, too, deserved this in your childhood but did not receive it. Many children of abuse have to learn what unconditional love looks like and may have trouble accepting it from another person because conditional love felt normal to them for so long. But it's worth it to strive for unconditional love because it comes with acceptance and a feeling of safety. You feel secure, knowing that even if something goes wrong or there are disagreements, there is always a safe place to go.

MISPLACED GUILT & SHAME

Primary effects of abuse that are not always addressed are the shame and guilt felt by the victims. Many children do not talk about the abuse when they are children because they are afraid of the outcome or of not being believed. When we finally admit it, usually later in life, there are feelings of being afraid or even embarrassed. Many people feel better getting it out and finally telling someone about their childhood; however, they still have trouble shaking those feelings that they did something wrong. It is important to talk about the difference between **guilt and shame** and how it is possible for abuse victims to actually feel both.

Guilt: *a feeling after you've done something wrong or perceived you did something wrong* (Salters-Pedneault, 2021).

Shame: *a feeling that your whole self is wrong; may not be related to something specific* (Salters-Pedneault, 2021).

The distinction between these two is palpable. Guilt is not always felt after you have done something wrong, but it can also be felt when you have only perceived that to be true. For children, they may think the abuse is a result of something bad they did when in reality, there is **absolutely nothing** children could have done to warrant it! This happens especially if there are consequences for the abuser. A child might feel bad for telling someone and "getting the abuser in trouble." As for the shame you may feel, this could be unresolved feelings about your childhood in general. Many people report knowing that something was wrong as a child, but they couldn't place their finger on it. Now, as an adult, they realize what they endured was not normal or healthy. These feelings likely affect the way you communicate and handle other interpersonal relationships. If you do feel this way, please know that what happened to you was never and will never be your fault. Consulting a therapist or psychologist can help you to process these feelings and better understand why you feel this way. They can provide clarity on the situation to further affirm that you were not in the wrong.

CHAPTER SUMMARY

- In a dysfunctional family dynamic, there are five common types of dysfunctional households. Within these families, children will take on various roles from the peacekeeper to the rebel in order to distract and diffuse the toxic situation.
- Over time, emotional abuse will have effects on a child. This often happens in three ways: **behavioral, emotional, and mental**.
- Many childhood abuse victims have misplaced shame and guilt that carries into their adulthood unless dealt with.

In the next chapter, you will learn the importance of breaking the toxic abuse cycle so you can live a healthier life within yourself and within your relationships with your own children.

6

BREAKING THE TOXIC CYCLE

Now that we understand just how detrimental emotionally immature and abusive parents can be to a child's development, it's time for you to make the mature decision to break the toxic cycle here. Ask yourself, How do you wish your parents treated you?

The Golden Rule: *Treat your children and others the way you would have liked to be treated by your parents!*

It can be difficult to know exactly what this will look like since you did not have any kind of model growing up, but try and start with love. If you treat your child and others with love, then you will get that same love in return. Everything we say and do is watched carefully by our children. They are unable to separate good from bad or right from wrong. They are only able to repeat!

This is what becomes their normal. This is how we repeat the cycle **OR** break it. It is hard to do this. I won't lie to you! It will be frustrating and tiring. This "normal" pattern of abuse actually may feel comfortable to you, since it is all you know. But I can promise you that it will be more tiring to live this kind of life all over again with your own children. There are two ways that our history can impact us:

1. *Repeating what we know.*
2. *Driving us to push hard against it and change course.*

Know that once you break this toxic cycle, you will be ending the legacy of pain and abuse that may have started generations before you. This gives you an opportunity for a depth of love and nurturing that will have the power to enrich your life and those in it.

STOP THE TOXIC MESSAGES

It is up to us to stop the messages we learned in our own childhood. We have to unlearn these toxic patterns in order to formulate new and healthier ones. But first, we have to recognize what the most common toxic messages are. Let's take a look at what they are and then how we can *counter* them with a positive message.

1. "I never knew a good parent, so how can I be one?" vs. **"I know what a good parent isn't, which is just as powerful."**

- A central theme of this book is that you don't always have to know exactly how to move forward and break the cycle, but you have to know what direction you don't want to go in! That direction is backwards. You may be afraid of how to parent your own children but your internal compass can guide you by reminding you of what definitely didn't work during your childhood. Throughout our parenting journey, things take shape and grow. Wisdom is gained through experience. The difference between a good and bad parent is that the former is open to that experience! A good parent can recognize that they don't know everything, but they are willing to learn. You know how your parents made you feel; simply by making the decision not to treat your children in the same manner places you far ahead in your journey.

2. "Kids must be good to be loved." vs. **"No one is perfect. But my kids are always enough."**

- We are all humans! Everyone makes mistakes

and takes time to learn, especially children. They are still growing, formulating their own thoughts and opinions, and understanding how the world functions. This is why *patience* is such a crucial trait for a parent to have. It can be more difficult to be kind and compassionate toward the people you are closest to because you know how they can be. But having the expectation that mistakes will be made can set you up to be more patient and loving toward your children. This will be a different feeling, as your parents likely shamed you or became enraged whenever you acted "bad," so remind yourself of how this made you feel and do your best to behave in the opposite manner with your kids. You should never have been put down and it likely still affects you to this day. Your **inner voice**, which will be discussed in later chapters, is more negative than it should be. We can be critical of ourselves, but when our parents teach us that it's never okay to make a mistake, then we will be extra hard on ourselves.

3. "Disagreements are a bad sign. Everything should be perfect." vs. **"Disagreements are a normal part of relationships, and nothing will be perfect all the time."**

- Any kind of healthy relationship has room for disagreements and independent thought. *Love does not require complete compliance or submission.* In a strong, nurturing relationship, differences should be embraced! Your children are unique. Your own parents may have put down your opinions or differences but in a healthy dynamic, you want to foster these variances! As you get older, you may have anxiety surrounding disagreements with people in general. This is due to the *conditional* love you received from your parents. Your children deserve to be loved and cared for no matter what kinds of arguments or disagreements you may have.

4. "Kids should be seen and not heard." vs. **"Everyone has a voice and the right to speak up."**

- The phrase "kids should be seen and not heard" dates back to the 15th century. Obviously, things have changed and it is definitely out of date. It's important for your children to feel comfortable enough around you to speak up and tell you what's on their mind. We cannot be around our kids 24/7, as much as we would like to. They will have their own life when they leave the house. Therefore, it will be hard to always protect them. We can do our best to prepare them for the world, but we can also help by ensuring they know they can tell us anything. We should be asking what they need and how things are going in their daily life. If they feel comfortable in their right to speak up, then we can do a better job as parents to protect them and be aware of the people, events, and emotions they are facing in their independent world.

5. *"Kids must do what they are told."* vs. **"I will nurture self-respect and independent thought in my children."**

- Has your child ever said "no" to you? This can be upsetting, especially when you are asking them to do something specific; however, you need to be careful with your response. During your childhood, things likely went whichever way your parents wanted them to and that was that! But with your own children, the word "no" is something they should feel confident and strong about using. Of course, we need to implement rules and boundaries for what they are allowed to say "no" to, but it is a good sign when your children begin asserting themselves in this way.

6. *"What the kids want doesn't matter."* vs. **"Children matter and their needs matter."**

- During your childhood, you likely felt unimportant. This message may have been received through a variety of channels such as yelling, criticism, put-downs, or neglect. You may have given up on having needs or expressing them to your parents because you knew they would not be addressed or even acknowledged. You do not want this for your kids! When needs are not met, this can actually lead to a malnourished emotional and physical self, causing both physical and mental health illnesses. It also teaches the kids that the needs of other people matter, but theirs do not. This can lead them to form further unhealthy attachments.

7. *"It's not criticism, just discipline."* vs. **"If it is harmful or hurtful, it is not discipline."**

- And speaking of criticism or put-downs, you likely endured much of this from your parents! However, they may have excused it, calling it "discipline" that you deserved for something you did. Discipline actually comes from the word "disciple" which means to teach. Therefore, when you discipline your children, you should be teaching them a valuable lesson, not putting them down. In dysfunctional family households, children are always walking around on eggshells, worried about the next punishment when everything will go wrong again. The dynamic is fragile, and they feel a desperate need for control. When your children make a mistake, this is a great opportunity for you to show them that they will not always be perfect, *but that's okay.* Even when they do something wrong, you still love them and it does not mean they deserve to be shamed. This way, you will be influencing their inner life and how they treat their own shortcomings in the future. You can even involve them in the process of their consequences or reparations by asking them how they think they should fix a situation. This allows them the opportunity to use problem-solving skills and develop coping mechanisms for the next time something similar occurs.

8. *"Kids should never fly off the handle."* vs. **"Children need to express their feelings and sometimes their emotions will be strong."**

- Because children are still developing, they do not always know how to properly process their emotions. In order to understand them, they first must experience them! As the parent, you must give them a safe space to do so. Many children with emotionally immature parents are never given the space to do this and end up developing emotional troubles relating to social and intimate relationships. All emotions: happiness, sadness, anger, jealousy, and so on are a crucial part of development. When your child starts to express these feelings, you can help guide them. In a non-judgmental and safe environment, your children will be able to learn how to appropriately react to these emotions instead of feeling like they have to control and repress themselves in order to appease a parent. If they do lose control, have a temper tantrum, or are frustrated, you can help them process these emotions in a healthy way and discuss ways they can express them in a different way next time.

9. *"Children have no control of their life. Parents control them."* vs. **"Children can shape their own world and discover what works best for them."**

- In dysfunctional family households, *control* is owned by the parents. The children sway along with whatever decisions are being made on any given day, trying not to set the parents off. They adapt quickly to the toxic environment, understanding that they are not in control of what happens. Instead of asserting control over your children in a demanding and harmful way, you want to show them that they are safe and cared for. They will push against change sometimes, which is completely normal! Know that this is a good sign that shows they are not living in the same dysfunctional environment you had to endure. There is only so much anyone can control about their life. Be patient in your parenting journey and control what you can.

10. "If they act out, it is my fault because everything is always my fault." vs. **"They will grow and learn and you cannot do it for them."**

- As we discussed in the previous chapter, shame and guilt accompany children of abuse throughout their life. This is something you may have to continue dealing with even when you have your own children. You may take on the feelings of your children when they make a mistake and feel guilty for it. But this is a normal part of their growth! They have to stumble along the way in order to learn how to pick themselves back up. *This does not make you a bad parent and it does not mean it is your fault.* It's okay when things are messy. Do not worry about what other people think about the imperfections of your parenting. As long as you are doing the best you can do and are open to learning, you are already a great parent. Other people will always have opinions and suggestions, but only you know what is best for your child!

PREVENTING UNHEALTHY ATTACHMENTS

In the previous chapter, we discussed *attachment theory* and how often unhealthy attachments are formed in a dysfunctional family household. Another type of unhealthy attachment we want to avoid is *codependency*.

Codependency: a *mental, emotional, physical, and/or spiritual reliance on a partner, friend, or family member* (Gould, 2020).

Codependency is regularly associated with romantic relationships, but it can also form in friendships and family dynamics. It was originally coined in 1905 by Alcoholics Anonymous. It was used to define partners of individuals who engaged in alcohol abuse who enabled their behavior (Gould, 2020). This is still true today; however, it has a broader definition now. While codependency is not a formally categorized personality disorder, it does incorporate aspects of *attachment theory* patterns that develop early in childhood and overlap with other diagnosed personality disorders, such as *dependent personality disorder*.

This type of relationship is circular, as one person needs the other, who in turn, feels a need to be needed. The codependent person is often referred to as *"the giver,"* and feels low self-worth unless they are needed by *"the taker"* or the enabler. The needs of the taker are often prioritized and the giver has to keep on giving, often at their own sacrifice. Let's take a look at some signs of codependency:

- *A feeling of walking on eggshells to avoid conflict.*
- *Checking in with the other person to ask permission.*
- *Apologizing even if you've done nothing wrong.*
- *Trying to rescue or change the other person.*
- *Doing anything for the other person, even sacrificing your own morals, needs or goals.*
- *A need for people to like you.*
- *Difficulty finding time to be alone.*
- *A feeling like you've lost your sense of self.*
- *Excusing/feeling sorry for the other person when they do harmful things to you.*

This type of parent-child dynamic often carries on into adulthood and the child continues to try to please the emotionally immature parent within their codependent dynamic. This will be addressed in Chapter Eight when we discuss how you can free yourself from this toxic cycle. While we all feel responsible and care for family members, it becomes extremely unhealthy when our identity is defined by someone else. ***The result of this dynamic forming is never the fault of the child.***

A codependent parent will form an unhealthy attachment to their child and try to assert control over the child's life because of that attachment (Lewis, 2020). *This parent-child codependency is emotionally abusive.* The child learns that how they feel and what they need are not important. Instead, they must provide for their parents. This strips away their chance of forming their own unique personality and identity. A child's identity is formed through choices and experiences. When an emotionally immature parent prevents this by deciding what choices they make and what experiences they are allowed to have, the child can never think for themselves. They will also mimic their parents' behaviors, repeating the toxic cycle of abuse.

At this point, you are probably wondering: *How can I stop this?*

You have already taken the first step by recognizing what happened to you in your childhood. Next, you must focus on your own self-awareness. It is likely you haven't had a chance to do this much, since all of your focus was on your codependent parent. Engaging in the following behaviors can help you:

- *Stop self-criticizing.*
- *Separate yourself from the relationship by seeking outside activities.*

- *When worrying about someone else or the codependent, turn your concern inward.*
- *Be patient with yourself.*
- *Stand up for yourself when someone criticizes or belittles you.*
- *Don't be afraid to say "no."*
- *Consider therapy or a support group.*

Becoming self-aware will help you to not only separate yourself from the codependent bond with your emotionally immature parent that may still be strong, but it will also prevent you from repeating the same unhealthy attachment with your own children. When you can recognize your own tendencies, whether they are healthy or unhealthy, you can begin to put the needs of your children first and assess if the way you are treating them is similar to or different from your experience in childhood.

CHILDREN AS SPONGES

If you find that your children are misbehaving or acting out, there is always a reason behind this. *They crave and need your love and attention.* Children do not process their feelings in the same way adults do since they are still learning how to handle their emotions and develop their understanding of their individual selves. If we cannot meet their need for love and attention, they will eventually find other, unhealthy ways to meet their unmet needs. This can be in the form of acting out, withdrawing, or hanging out with problematic peers. Regardless of how your child chooses to express their negative feelings, if they are not addressed and handled, then they can develop long-lasting bad habits that they will continue into their adult years. Think of your own childhood. *Did you get into trouble often in school? Were you extremely quiet in an effort to not upset others? Did you have trouble making friends and expressing yourself?* It may be difficult to remember now, but the trauma of your childhood certainly affected you.

Children are aware of and can sense much more than we give them credit for. They are **emotional sponges**, constantly picking up on and absorbing our behaviors, patterns, and emotional states. When they can sense how we are feeling, they may take on these feelings as well. You may think they don't know that you are stressed about the important presentation you have at work or about the argument you had with your spouse. And this is true! However, they can feel the tension and they don't know what's causing it. *Therefore, they will assume they did something wrong to cause this because they cannot possibly understand the full complexities of life.* It is critical to understand that it all can start and end with you, the parent. It is during childhood that these toxic patterns begin developing. Before you even think that your behavior could possibly affect the child, they are already suffering. Decide to be a positive model for your child. Be open and honest with your children, and in turn, they will do the same for you.

DEVELOP A LOGICAL NARRATIVE OF YOUR STORY

If you are reading this book, it is more than likely that you endured some kind of childhood abuse at the hands of emotionally immature parents. However, your experience is completely unique from that of someone else. We have discussed common phrases, traits, and types of emotionally immature parents, but your particular experience is **only yours**. No one else lived it and no one else felt or experienced the trauma that you did.

Many people live with this unresolved trauma throughout their life and even as they take steps to ensure it does not happen again, they still tiptoe around the actual story behind it all. You can live a happier, healthier life by facing the full pain of your own childhood and creating a true, honest account of your childhood that makes sense to you. This will help you connect more with your inner self. Ultimately, this will help you become a far better parent through the example you set. This means you will have to see your parents as human beings with flaws and imperfections. You do not have to wallow or blame, but you can gain a better understanding of why you are the way you are today and resolve issues that continue to influence your behavior. By reading this book, you can already start identifying those negative patterns and work to stop them before they get out of hand. You have the power to choose how you want your relationship to be with your children, rather than letting your childhood dictate your future.

WHEN TO SEEK HELP

If you feel that you are still at risk of repeating toxic and abusive patterns, seeking professional help is your best option. You can do this by looking for an experienced therapist who will help you identify triggers from your past. This in itself can be an enlightening experience, as anger and confusion stemming from your childhood may still be driving your actions. Once they identify triggers, the therapist can teach you proven techniques for dealing with them in a healthy way. They will guide you in the examination of your past and teach you coping mechanisms to move forward. One of the most common forms of therapy for addressing traumatic events is **cognitive-behavioral therapy (CBT).**

Cognitive-Behavioral Therapy (CBT): *a type of psychotherapeutic treatment that helps people learn how to identify and change destructive or disturbing thought patterns that have a negative influence on behavior and emotions* (Cherry, 2021).

CBT works to change our automatic thoughts that contribute to negative moods and actions. It is about more than just identifying the patterns. It also focuses on the strategies to overcome them. As stated previously in this chapter, a great parent is open to learning and changing behavior for the benefit of their child. Understanding how to be positive is important and you shouldn't feel like you've failed as a parent because you decide to go to therapy. Working toward a healthier life is a great step that you should be proud of taking for your family.

CHAPTER SUMMARY

- It can be difficult to know exactly how to parent your own children, since you did not have any kind of model growing up, but try and start with love. Treat your children the same way you wish your parents treated you.

- It is up to us to stop the messages we learned during our own childhood. We have to unlearn these toxic patterns in order to formulate new, healthier ones.
- Another type of unhealthy attachment we want to avoid is codependency. A codependent parent will form an unhealthy attachment to their child and try to assert control over the child's life because of that attachment. *This parent-child codependency is emotionally abusive.*
- A great parent is open to learning and changing behaviors for the benefit of their child. Understanding how to be positive is important and you shouldn't feel like you've failed as a parent because you decide to go to therapy.

In the next chapter, you will learn how to stop feeling guilty if you are still feeling unhappy during your healing process.

7

FEELING MISERABLE WHEN I SHOULD BE HAPPY

Now that you are an adult and are no longer under the control of your parents, *do you feel happy?* Many people cannot answer yes to this question. And **there is nothing wrong with that!** Healing from emotionally abusive parents can be a long process and you should not feel any guilt or shame about being unhappy, even if you feel that you have nothing to be unhappy about! Allow yourself to put the guilt and shame away. You have been feeling these negative emotions for too long already.

It's true that none of us really know what is going on in another person's life. We all have our own internal struggles that are not visible to people around us, regardless of how close we may feel to them. It's normal to feel confused and frustrated about your unhappy feelings since now you may feel you don't "deserve" to feel bad. Remember, the first relationships we have are with our parents. If you were raised by emotionally immature parents, then there is a **deep ache** within you that you continue to silently struggle with alone. *This is, of course, not your fault, but it is your responsibility to heal from this damage.* If not, then you may be facing a life of unhappiness and a feeling of helplessness surrounding this ache within you.

There is good news, however. You can take control of your life and your story and decide the course of your life going forward. There was only so much you could do as a child, but now you can feel a sense of empowerment in knowing that the helpless time you endured is over and your life is under the control of no one else but *you*. This is your opportunity to "re-raise" yourself with the empathy, kindness, safety, and support that your parents were unable to provide you.

WHAT HEALING DOES NOT LOOK LIKE

Knowing what healing doesn't look like is just as important as knowing what it does. In order for you to recover from the damage caused during your childhood, you have to **repair your reality.** As we learned in Chapter Five, the emotional abuse and manipulation tactics used by your parents had an effect on your brain structure and emotional development. Your perception has been damaged by your experience. It's crucial to recognize that healing does not look like the following:

- **Changing Oneself:** In order to re-raise yourself and heal from the abuse, you do not have to change who you are. You are a unique individual and we are all a product of our experiences and background. This does not make us any more special than the next person. It does, however, help define us and shape our personalities. You do not have to change anything about your personality during your healing process. *Healing should be all about you, but not about changing yourself.* Instead of changing yourself, you want to know yourself better. You can learn to recognize your triggers, which are the things that remind you of your childhood experience and make you upset, and learn to trust your intuition.
- **Fixing Your Parents:** This will be discussed further in the next chapter, but it is not your job to fix your parents. Now that you are armed with knowledge from this book, it may be tempting to use it against your parents. But this will do nothing to help your healing. Your healing is about you and as much as you might

think helping your parents will help, it is always better to focus on what you are certain you can change and control. And that is only you!

- **A Smooth Ride**: Healing will not be a smooth ride. I am here to tell you the truth in this book. It will be an emotional rollercoaster. You will have days when you feel strong and completely healed. Then, the pendulum will swing and you will feel unhappy again. This is completely normal and healthy. An emotionally abusive childhood creates feelings of confusion and emotional instability. When you begin the healing process, you are going to be confronting some heavily repressed emotions head on, and this will be difficult. However, it will be worth it in the end.

HEALING MANTRAS

Your mind may cloud easily or get distracted by negative thoughts during the healing process. In this case, *mantras*, or phrases that you can repeat to yourself, are a great way to stay focused on your end goal. Everything carries weight, especially the thoughts you hold about yourself and the way you speak about yourself. We know this from childhood because the mental and emotional abuse from our parents has impacted us greatly and continues to even now. But we can also use the power of words for healing. Through the use of these positively inspired statements and phrases, you can work to free yourself of stress while healing. Mantras are simple and effective, and they help to keep you on track. Here are a few mantras that you may find useful:

"This too shall pass."

"My childhood was not my fault."

"I am enough just as I am."

"I choose to feel good today."

"Everything I need to heal is within myself."

You may wonder, *Do I really need to repeat these every day?* The short answer is no. But you should strongly consider doing so as often as possible. The toxic messages from your childhood were ingrained in you every day and now is the time for you to rewrite the narrative. After growing up with these messages, you must actively undo them. The above mantras are a great start but it's important for you to create one that ***holds meaning for you***. The priority is to have a strong, safe, and comforting voice that will guide you to healing.

FIXING YOUR ATTACHMENT STYLE

One of the main damages caused by an abusive mother is **attachment trauma.** In Chapter Five, we uncovered the different insecure attachment styles formed by emotionally immature parents. These alter how we interact with others in romantic, social, and familial relationships going forward. Healing from attachment trauma will take learning how to attach securely. To do so, you can follow the next several techniques. This chapter and the following will present to you the critical **8 Secure Attachment Techniques** that will help you form secure attachments, as you begin to heal from the attachment trauma you endured in childhood:

▷ **Technique #1: Develop your passions**.

Because you did not have the time as a child to grow and nurture your interests, you may be unaware of what you're passionate about. There is nothing wrong with this! Now is the time for you to cultivate new interests, hobbies, and pursuits. Sometimes, we discover our passions once we act on them and only then do we realize the things we truly care for.

▷ **Technique #2: Take some risks**

A certain amount of calculated risks will help you to find courage and rebuild your self-esteem. Once you do, you'll become more confident in your ability to adapt to change and try new things. You may even discover that you are stronger and more resilient than you think.

▷ Technique #3: Get physical

Moving your body helps exercise your mind. Your physical wellness can nurture your emotional health as well.

▷ Technique #4: Regulate self-talk

Our inner feelings tend to be harsh. We are usually our own worst critics! But becoming aware of this will help you instill new ideas and healthier thought patterns. Each time you recognize negative self-talk, ask yourself if you would talk to a best friend or someone else you loved that way. If you wouldn't, try to give yourself the same level of kindness you would give to someone else. Feeling shame and criticism from negative self-talk will not lead you towards recovery.

▷ Technique #5: Develop insight

Most of our inner and outer reactions since childhood are automatic. We did not have the time to develop a strong insight into our own needs, wants, and desires as children. Now is our time to do so. When healing, you want to think about why certain events occur and why you behave in certain ways. This is not to place blame or to self-criticize; it is to better understand yourself and the true depth of the scars left by your upbringing so you do not continue to repeat negative patterns.

All of us are hard-wired to attach to other human beings. This is why we cried when we were babies. We wanted to be closer to our mothers. Even those who feel they are completely independent may find themselves falling into some semblance of dependency once they enter a romantic relationship or a very close friendship because these intimate relationships subconsciously stimulate the attachment style we learned as children (Lancer, 2021). Through conscious effort, you can change your attachment style. You may even want to assess the attachment style of your partner or friend based on their behaviors and reactions to closeness. Seeking out a therapist can be helpful, as they will help you to work on insecurities. It can be extremely healing to seek relationships with those who have a secure attachment. If you know you are prone to an insecure style, you will certainly feel more stable with someone who has a secure attachment style.

Most importantly, go slow! Once you realize your attachment type may be insecure, take a cautious approach toward any kind of relationship you foster. This doesn't mean you have to shy away from people and be afraid to talk to others. It simply means that you should be aware and patient with yourself when communicating during the formation of new relationships. Strangely, this fact is true: *the more autonomous we are, the more we're capable of intimacy* (Lancer, 2021). Have you ever heard the phrase, "You can't love anyone else until you learn to love yourself"? This is prevalent in this situation. Until you heal your attachment trauma and find your own independence and *unconditional love* for yourself, you cannot yet attach to another person in a healthy way.

▷ **Technique #6: Acknowledging Your Inner Child**

Everyone has what is called an **inner child**. This looks slightly different for everyone, as you might see this as a representation of yourself from childhood, a combination of different stages of your growth, or a symbol of your youthfulness (Raypole, 2021). An awareness of this can help you acknowledge those pieces of yourself that are broken and need healing. For people who did not endure an abusive childhood, their inner child is

132 | VANESSA A. P.

often the reminder of a carefree, joyful time and chan-
neling it can help them deal with any challenging times
they may currently be facing. But for those who had a
difficult childhood filled with emotional abuse, neglect,
and trauma, your inner child may be in need of protection and comfort (Raypole, 2021).

Throughout this book, we have learned that we cannot
suppress our pain. That ache inside of us is not going
away unless we face it head on. If we don't, it will
surface in our life through mental illness, negative
attachments, unhealthy habits, or substance abuse. It is
up to us to heal. It can take time, but by first acknowledging the presence of our inner child, we can begin to
explore our relationship with them. If you're feeling
doubtful about delving into the past, you may have a
harder time with this healing process. It can be terri-
fying to think of opening yourself up to memories,
emotions, and trauma that happened years ago but try
to look at it as a process of self-discovery. The more
you know yourself, the better you can understand why
certain things happened in your life or why you
continue to feel negative emotions.

To start, try and think of a few instances from your
childhood that may have been hurtful. You likely still
carry the pain from these today. For some people, this
in itself can be soothing when they open the door to

their inner child and give them a chance to speak their mind. But doing so can also trigger strong emotions and old wounds (Raypol, 2021). You might notice any of the following:

- Anger
- Guilt/shame
- Vulnerability
- Insecurity
- Abandonment/rejection

By tracing these feelings back to a particular childhood instance, you can begin to draw similarities to situations in your adulthood that trigger the same responses. Let's look at an example:

Example: Rachel's anniversary is on Friday night and she and her husband planned the whole evening. She has been excited for weeks. Her husband works a demanding job with long hours and he has been telling her how he is looking forward to spending time with her. But that day, she gets a call from him that he has to stay at work longer than expected and won't be able to make it to their dinner reservation, but he will be home right after. She feels rejected and abandoned. She hangs up on him and throws a temper tantrum in their room, crying for the rest of the evening.

Through the eyes of her inner child, Rachel was being rejected by her husband. Though she knows he has a demanding job, she still feels abandoned. This may have connections to her childhood and her attachment style with her parents. Consider how you feel when a friend cancels a meeting or you feel let down. *Does this remind you of times when your parents didn't show up or made promises that they couldn't keep?* Listening to these feelings can help you to better understand your reactions and emotions within your current relationships.

TIPS FOR RECOVERY

There are many ways to begin your recovery journey from an abusive childhood. Recovery looks different for everyone and what works for someone else may not be as useful for you. In this section, we will discuss a list of tools that you can try to begin healing. As discussed, the primary damage you will need to heal from is that of attachment trauma. You must learn to attach in healthier ways moving forward in your relationships

- **Therapy:** Therapy has been largely talked about in the previous chapter. This is because it is such a great tool to help you better understand your childhood and keep everything straight in your head. It can be overwhelming trying to process everything yourself.

- **Support Groups:** These are great when you are trying not to do everything yourself. You want to be sure you have positive friends, family, or even a recovery group that you feel comfortable sharing with. This alone can make you feel better and less overwhelmed in your recovery process.
- **Positive Inner Voice:** Once you acknowledge your *inner child*, you can begin to change your internal voice to be more positive. This will help you be more patient and understanding with yourself, instead of being a harsh critic of everything you do.
- **Journals:** These are extremely useful tools to help you track your thought patterns. When you journal every day, you can keep track of not only how you are feeling day-to-day, but also what kind of thoughts are going through your mind in general. If you pair this with therapy or with a support group, you can begin to understand why these thoughts might be occurring.
- **Exercise**: This has been proven to improve both mental and emotional health. Exercise works to improve all areas of your health.

- **Religion**: While not everyone is religious, tapping into a higher being can help you to step outside your mind and focus on something greater. This can draw you out of a negative thought pattern, help you lead a healthier lifestyle, and focus on positive thoughts.
- **Recovery Resources (*Like this book!*)**: Reading all that you can about recovery, your childhood, and why you may feel the way you do now will only further your education on the subject. And as we know, knowledge is power! When you are able to fully appreciate your situation, you can work to change it for the better.
- **Repetition**: All of these tips must be done repeatedly! Recovery is a slow process and there will be mishaps. But if you continue to repeat the healthy steps and focus on healing your attachment trauma and becoming as healthy as you can be, you will succeed.

CHAPTER SUMMARY

- In order for you to recover from the damage caused during your childhood, you have to **repair your reality.**
- One of the main damages caused by an abusive mother is *attachment trauma.* Healing from

attachment trauma will take learning how to attach securely.

- An awareness of your inner child can help you acknowledge those pieces of yourself that are broken and need healing. For those who had a difficult childhood filled with emotional abuse, neglect, and trauma, your inner child may be in need of protection and comfort.

In the next chapter, you will learn how to take a healthy perspective of your relationship with your parents.

8

HOW CAN I STOP EXPECTING?

D o you find yourself still expecting your parents to change or act differently now that you are an adult living a life separate from them? This happens more often than not with adults who suffered child abuse at the hands of their emotionally immature parents. Or they are now able to see how wrong they were treated in their childhood, and they cannot believe their parents would still act in this manner. Either way, it can be a frustrating experience to watch your parents continue to behave in this toxic and harmful way. *So, what can we do about it?* The most realistic answer is *nothing.* It is not our job to change our parents! They are adults and can care for themselves. It is not your place to change them or to prove to them that what they did was wrong. This will only take more energy away from the positivity in your life.

Now, this does not mean you need to forget all that happened to you! You do not need to do this **but you do need to move forward**. This means that we have to stop expecting our parents to change. You might be reading this now and realizing for the first time just how long you've been waiting for your parents to change. It's a subconscious experience to simply wait for your parents to change, in the hopes that one day they may even apologize for what they've done. But because of who they are, it's crucial for your own well-being to accept that this will not happen and move forward with your own life.

TECHNIQUE #7: FINDING A HEALTHY DETACHMENT

Throughout our life, there are going to be people that we love and truly care for. However, we simply cannot give them too much of our emotional energy, otherwise, we will suffer for it. There are times when we must *let go. When you are around your parents, even now as an adult, do you feel emotionally drained?* This is where a healthy **detachment** can be especially helpful.

There are many reasons to detach from a relationship, such as physical or verbal abuse, stress or anxiety, and negativity. Regardless of the reason, detaching can help you let go in a way that works best for you.

Detachment: *being disconnected or disengaged from the feelings of other people* (Cherry, 2021).

Detachment can be experienced in different ways. It might mean avoiding your parents or being in certain situations with them that cause you anxiety and stress. These situations may often lead you to feel worse than you did when you first entered the interaction. Detachment might also mean building **boundaries**, which will be discussed later in this chapter.

Understanding what emotional detachment looks like is just as important as understanding what it does *not* look like. Being detached does not mean that you are unable to feel emotions or that you completely block them out. It also doesn't mean that you lack empathy! Instead, we want to focus on building up healthier boundaries and better understanding acceptable behaviors. Detaching from your relationship with your parents does not mean that you don't care about them. It only means that you need to take an emotional step back to evaluate how the relationship is affecting your personal health.

Do you worry about what your parents are thinking all of the time? Do you still feel like you need their approval or need to tell them what you are doing all of the time?

As a child, you likely took responsibility for their actions and handled the baggage of their emotions and yours. Now, as an adult, you can put an end to this emotional overload. Detaching can give you the space to do this and to heal from the emotional abuse.

TYPES OF BOUNDARIES

Many people believe they already have good boundaries in place when they do not. This is because they have either never explored just how many different types of boundaries there are, or because they have never had the chance to understand what is acceptable or not acceptable for them. **What is a boundary for you may not be a boundary for someone else.** And that is okay! You should never have to explain yourself when it comes to what you are comfortable with. Let's look at the different types of boundaries and examples first, and then we will discuss how you can begin to set boundaries in your own life (Earnshaw, 2019).

1. Physical: personal space, touch, and other physical needs such as resting, food, and water.

- *"No. Please don't touch me like that."*
- *"I am actually really tired and cannot come over now."*
- *"Please give me some space. I feel crowded."*

2. Emotional: feelings, energy, how much emotional energy you are taking in/sharing with others.

- *"I feel upset when you criticize my feelings. I will only share with you if you are respectful of how I feel."*
- *"I am sorry you feel that way. But I am not in a place right now to talk about that."*
- *"Right now is not a good time for me to talk about this with you. Can we talk about it later?"*

3. Time: understanding priorities, setting aside time for different areas of life, not overcommitting.

- *"I can't come over today because I have too much work to do."*
- *"I can talk, but only for an hour."*
- *"I would love to chat, but I don't want to overcommit myself. Can we do it another time?"*

4. Sexual: consent, respect, understanding preferences, privacy, agreement, trusting your partner.

- *"Is this comfortable?"*
- *"I actually do not like that. Let's try something else."*
- *"I do not want to have sex tonight."*

5. Intellectual: your ideas, curiosity, thoughts, respect for your own ideas and those of others.

- *"Please don't belittle me. It's okay for us to disagree."*
- *"We don't get very far when we talk about this, so I think we should change the conversation topic for now."*
- *"Let's respect our different opinions on this topic."*

6. Material: items, possessions such as your home, money, clothing, furniture, etc., an understanding of what you can or cannot share.

- *"I cannot lend you any money right now. I need it for my bills."*
- *"I would be happy to let you use my car, but I need it back by 5 o'clock."*
- *"Last time I lent you money, you did not give it back, therefore I cannot give you any more."*

Being able to set boundaries in these six areas will help you be successful in creating a detachment and a healthy emotional space. Without these in place, you may continue to experience feelings of violation, resentment, and more. It's always good to remember these boundaries in all areas of your life. Many of us remember to put these in place when it comes to our friends or co-workers, but it can be more difficult to do so with our own family.

TECHNIQUE #8: SETTING BOUNDARIES

Now that we have identified the different types of boundaries, we can begin to understand how to set them within our relationship with our parents. Depending on how often you see them, you may only need to implement this once a year, a few times a year, or every single day. But having a plan in place to deal with boundary violations when they happen (and they will!) can alleviate anxiety before it even happens. Let's look at the steps to set healthy boundaries:

Start by doing some **self-reflection**. This might seem like a minuscule step but it's good to take some time to understand what is important to you and why you want to set these boundaries. For children of emotionally immature parents, you might notice when your parents do certain things or say certain phrases to you, they bother you but you don't quite understand *why*. This is because a boundary of yours is being violated but you might not be able to identify exactly what boundary is being crossed. Taking the time to think about why their actions bother you can help you start to identify similar behaviors in other areas that you would also like to address.

Next, you want to start addressing this by **starting small.** You don't want to overwhelm yourself and start detaching or setting too many boundaries upfront because remember, you will have to enforce them! Therefore, start small and be patient with yourself. Maybe you notice that every time you speak to your mother on the phone in the morning, she puts you in a bad mood for the rest of the day. A good boundary here would be to tell her you can no longer talk on the phone in the morning and she will have to call you later in the day. This is something small and easier to enforce because if she does call, you can simply ignore it.

As you are doing this, you might notice your parents saying things or engaging in behaviors that cross your boundaries. When you notice these for the first time, **set a boundary right away**. This way, it does not become a "habitual boundary crossing" that will take longer for you to break over time. Once you've reflected on the first step, you will start noticing little things easier. If you cut it off right away, you will feel more confident and stop the problem before it begins.

Perhaps the most important thing to keep in mind throughout this process is **being consistent**. You cannot set a boundary one day, then let it slide the next. You must continue to encourage and foster these new expectations in your life and demand the respect you deserve from your parents if they are going to continue to be a part of your life. Consistency will help you to also reinforce your ideas in your own mind, reminding you of why you started this healing journey.

During this process, you must be open to **communicating** with your parents. These discussions should not be argumentative, but should instead be open and positive. While this may only be coming from your end, you can make the decision to raise your concerns in a healthy way and not react to them if they look for a confrontation.

And don't forget to **cheer yourself on**! This is such an important step you've taken in your life, and you should commend yourself for it. You've decided to do the right thing for your own health and stick up for what your personal boundaries are. You have to show love to yourself because if you don't believe you deserve positivity and healthy boundaries, then you are not going to work hard to put them in place. Much of this process comes down to the self-worth you hold. This might seem like a daunting prospect but the more you encourage the mindset within yourself, the easier the actual experience will be.

CONSEQUENCES OF BOUNDARY VIOLATIONS

So, what do I do if/when my parents do not respect my new boundaries? Sadly, your parents will not like most of the boundaries you put in place. This is because they prevent them from having control over you and especially *from making everything about them.* They won't be able to suck the positivity out of you the way they would like to. Instead, they will be met with an emotional blocker when they try to do so. But if they continue to push and ignore the boundaries you put in place, there will have to be ***consequences***.

Now, this might seem flipped! You might be wondering, am I supposed to use consequences as the "child" in this situation? Because you are now an adult and much more mature than your own parents, you can absolutely use consequences. There are many ways to do this and you will be able to gauge what works best for you once a boundary is violated. Here are some consequences for your parents when boundary violations happen.

- **Take away something they want:** While this sounds much like a punishment meant for a

LIFE AFTER EMOTIONALLY IMMATURE PARENTS | 149

child, it can be used in this scenario as well. When a boundary is crossed, you can put an end to something that you know your parents want. It must be something they really want because otherwise, they won't feel that there is any consequence for their actions. Then, they may be prone to do it all over again.

*Example: Anna's mother always drops by her house. She never calls, despite Anna repeatedly asking her to do so. She comes by the house at all hours of the day and gives no regard to Anna's **time boundaries**, showing up when she has friends over or when her children are in the middle of doing their homework. Sometimes she will even come to the house when Anna's family is not home. Her mother has a key to the house that she asked for "in case of emergencies" but uses for everything. When her mother comes over in the middle of dinner, Anna asks for the key to her house. Her mother gets extremely upset and throws the key down on the table, then storms out.*

In this example, a clear boundary violation was happening. Anna's mother reacted negatively, but this is not Anna's fault! She had to set this boundary in order to respect her own time boundaries. By taking away her mother's key, she is showing her that she is not welcome to simply come and go as she pleases. After verbally setting her boundary, Anna had to create a consequence when her mother was unable to respect it.

- **Allow for natural consequences**: Sometimes there are natural consequences that occur without your interference when a boundary crossing takes place. Many people without boundaries will lose relationships, get in trouble with the law, and may be in deep financial debt as a result of the lack of inner boundaries as well. Let these consequences happen because the only way for them to see the effect of their behavior is for them to deal with it. There will not be much effort on your part for these natural consequences to take place, as they usually take the form of reactions from others.

*Example: John's mother attends all of her grandson's baseball games. She yells from the stands and is very obnoxious. John tells his mother that Henry doesn't like it when she does this because it embarrasses him in front of his friends. She ignores John and continues to do it anyway, violating **emotional and intellectual boundaries**. She cheers for Henry when he does well and berates him when he strikes out or misses a catch. Eventually, Henry quits baseball and tells his father it's because he doesn't want his grandmother yelling at him from*

LIFE AFTER EMOTIONALLY IMMATURE PARENTS | 151

the stands. He also stops going over to her house and won't talk to her when she calls him.

In this scenario, we see John attempting to set a boundary with his mother. He tells her that Henry does not like it when she yells at him from the stands. It is inappropriate for her to do so and it belittles him in front of his peers. The natural consequence was for her to lose her relationship with Henry. If she cannot repair the relationship by accepting healthier boundaries, then she will not have a relationship with her grandson.

- **Preserve the good things about the relationship**: If you still have your parents in your life, then there are certainly things that are good within the relationship. Things may not be all bad all the time. If you want to continue a relationship with your parents, then you will certainly want to keep these good things in place. Therefore, while putting consequences in place for things that aren't working, you want to be sure to preserve the things that are working! If you were to use these good things as consequences, it would damage the relationship deeply instead of allowing for an opportunity to heal.

152 | VANESSA A. P.

Example: Every Sunday, Gianna and her father have coffee. They have been doing this since she moved out two years ago. However, her father also used to stop by unannounced, demand that she sees him multiple times a week, and constantly call her when she first left. He was not respecting her **time boundaries** *until she put up a boundary and told him that she would only be able to commit to seeing him for their weekly coffee on Sundays.*

In this situation, Gianna was able to preserve her Sunday coffee with her overbearing father by putting a boundary in place for his other demands. This way, her energy was not drained by him and she, too, could continue to look forward to their coffee together on Sunday mornings.

Regardless of how you choose to make consequences for your parents when they violate a boundary, it is clear that the consequence must *matter*. If your parents do not care about the consequences, they won't change their behavior. Also, if they do not care about preserving the relationship, they also will keep attempting to violate the boundary. Keep in mind that you may have to use consequences for many different boundary violations in your relationship with your parents. But trust me, it will be worth it! It will reduce your stress and the anxiety surrounding the relationship, allowing you to have a new, healthier dynamic between you and your parents.

NEW RELATIONSHIP, OLD PARENTS

What would happen if instead of seeing your parents as the parents, you saw them as children? How would you treat the relationship differently? How would you treat them differently?

Changing the way you view your parents will help you change your own **expectations**. This is a great way to deal with toxic people. You might wonder why you feel ridiculous to expect something normal, such as kindness or respect, from your parents. Both these things you would easily find in a normal, healthy relationship. *This is because you know that you deserve this but you also know that your parents won't provide it for you.* As a grown adult, you are still holding out for what you deserve, assuming they should and will give it to you. But there is no way to change how someone else behaves. There is only a way to change your expectations. We will discuss how to do so in the next section but for now, let's discuss five ways you can begin to cultivate a newer relationship with your parents today:

1. **Focus on issues, not one another**: Using the above boundary examples and consequences,

you can bring issues to the attention of your parents and tell them what needs to change. This should happen without fingers being pointed or any blame given. You want to put an emphasis on fixing the issues, not the person. This way, there is a separation there, and the relationship itself can stand strong, while the issue is something that needs to be worked on.

2. **Ease back in**: If you and your parents have been estranged, or have a strained relationship, ease back into it slowly! You don't want to all of the sudden start seeing them all of the time and allowing them into every aspect of your life. You want to ensure that you are ready emotionally for the change and you can establish the relationship at your own pace.

3. **Look within**: Maybe there are some things about yourself that you want to work on. We all have strengths and weaknesses, especially when it comes to communication within relationships. Take a look within yourself and see what things you would like to work on that could help your relationships. This does not only apply to your parents, but also to others close to you.

4. **Be honest**: This step is mostly for yourself. You want to be honest with yourself about why you

want a healthier relationship with your parents. Are you looking to set a good example for your own children? Have you always wanted to mend the relationship? Are you expecting something out of it? Whatever the reason, honesty is the only way you will be able to move forward in a healthy manner.

5. **Be patient**: Fixing a strained relationship will not be easy. Starting a new relationship with your parents sounds great but it won't be so easy! You will have to adjust your perspective, stand strong and be patient with both them and yourself throughout the whole process.

RELEASING YOUR EXPECTATIONS

The way that we view the world, other people, and ourselves is due, at least in part, to our own expectations. They affect our experiences and influence the way we react to situations in our daily life. By refocusing and changing our expectations, we can begin to better control our own perspective. You may be wondering, in what areas of my life can I do this? Almost every interaction we have gives us an opportunity to formulate our own belief systems. It is through these belief systems that we create our own sets of expectations. In order to release these expectations, you can try any of the following:

- **"Empty cup" approach**: This approach centers around the belief that we should come to every situation with an "empty cup" ready to receive information. When dealing with our emotionally immature parents, our cup may already be full or we may already be expecting something negative. We become so accustomed to the way our parents behave that it's natural to expect a particular reaction from them. But if we try to approach each interaction with them from an "empty cup" perspective, we can resist interjecting past experience and see the situation uniquely on its own.

- **Be present**: Along the same lines of the empty cup approach, being present can help ground us into what is currently happening around us. You want to be present with your parents in the *now*, not in the past. Being stuck in the past can cloud your judgment and reactions to current life events. You are reacting based on past situations. This does not mean you need to forget all that happened in the past but it does mean that you are giving each new situation with your parents a chance in order to foster a new kind of relationship with them.

- **Check reality**: This is an important way to gauge whether what you believe about another person in a situation matches the current reality. Even though you know who your parents are, it's good to take a step back from how disappointing they are and make sure you are looking at them from a realistic place. Often, we react emotionally rather than by using our judgment. If a situation is causing you intense, negative emotions, it may be good to take a step back and return to it at a later time with a clear head.

- **Let go of fantasies**: A running theme throughout this chapter is to let go of any fantasies you may still hold about your parents. Freeing yourself of these expectations from your parents takes the pressure off and allows you to remain realistic. You don't want to go into every single interaction with your parents expecting *something*, whether that be the same old thing or hoping for something better.

THE GREY ROCK TECHNIQUE

Imagine that you are a grey rock. Just a simple, forgettable, grey rock, similar to countless other grey rocks nearby.

This is how you begin the grey rock technique. By using this technique, you make yourself boring and uninteresting to a manipulative individual. This way, you give them nothing to feed off of. This means no information, no drama, and no way for them to attempt to control you. This technique can be especially effective for dealing with parents who cannot seem to respect your boundaries but whom you also cannot avoid.

Many of us have similar situations with people in our lives. Maybe you have family members that you do not personally have any kind of close relationship with but you cannot avoid them. You see them at family functions, over at other family members' homes, and at family reunions. This may be the type of relationship you have with your parents. There could be a million reasons why you cannot or do not want to completely cut off your parents from your life. In order to be a grey rock, it's crucial to follow the steps to ensure that you are disengaging from the interaction in a way that will give your parents nothing to try to use against you.

First, you want to **offer nothing** to the conversation. Your parents likely thrived on chaos throughout your childhood and they probably still do now! During any necessary interactions with them, you want to have a blank face, show no reaction, and reply with simple words such as "yes" or "no" or even "uh-huh." This will show them how disinterested you are in what they have to say. This means that you will also tell them nothing about what you are doing. Maybe you would have previously filled them in on your regular life events but now you are going to refrain from doing this completely. If they do ask about something, you can respond with, "That is personal."

Your body language will say a lot about how you are feeling toward the conversation as well. This is why you will want to focus on avoiding eye contact, as this is known to facilitate emotional connection. Not only this but **disengaging** in this manner will help *reinforce your sense of detachment.* It can keep you focused on other, more positive things around you instead of their attempts at manipulation. This can be upsetting for the toxic person and if you find your parent getting upset, you will have to stay strong. You do not want to show them any kind of body language that shows you are upset. They may be simply looking for a reaction from you, regardless of what kind of reaction that is. Because they are emotionally immature, they want any kind of attention and if you appear to be negatively reacting to them, this is still something for them to absorb.

Because these interactions need to be handled with care, they should also be **as short as possible.** Again, if you must talk with your parents, talking over the phone or text would be a good way to handle it. Simply answer their questions with short responses, then exit the interaction. Perhaps most important of all is to **refrain from telling them that you are grey rocking**. They might notice you are not telling them anything and seem disinterested in interacting with them. This may cause them to confront you. This is a time when you should not be honest with them. They do not deserve any explanation for the actions you take in order to preserve your own sanity and well-being. Also, they may try to use the knowledge of your technique to further manipulate or control you.

WHEN TO CUT THEM OFF

Cutting anyone out of our lives is a difficult process, but when they are your parent, this can be a deep, painful process. *So, how do you know when it's time to cut them out of your life for good?* As discussed in previous sections of this chapter, it can sometimes be enough to take a new perspective on the relationship, set boundaries, and limit contact with your parents in order to save the relationship. But that is not always enough and at some points, the overall impact of the emotionally immature parent can simply become too destructive.

Cutting off your parents will be a decision you need to make and in order to break the cycle of abuse, it may be necessary. If you feel that you are still stuck in the cycle, always feeling off and upset after interactions with them, it may be time, especially if you notice the following two aspects in your relationship:

1. *A consistent disregard for boundaries.*
2. *Emotional drain.*

These two negative aspects alone are enough to impact your physical, mental, and emotional well-being. You may have children of your own and you want to set a positive example for them. If they are around the relationship between you and your parents and they are witnessing a lack of boundaries and you becoming emotionally drained, you can be certain they are receiving the wrong message. This will affect their *attachment style*. You definitely don't want this! Only you will know when, if ever, it's time to cut off your emotionally immature parents but keep a lookout for the above two warning signs.

SHIFT THE FOCUS BACK TO YOU

This chapter tackles a lot of information on how to manage our expectations of our parents *but what about our expectations of ourselves?* There is only so much you can control in this world, and you are the only thing that you have complete control over. The process of healing after the cycle of abuse is one that takes a long time. It is a learning process. You will uncover things about yourself that you never knew, find new boundaries to put in place that will lead you to healthier attachment styles, and have to deal with uncertainty.

All of this is normal. What's important is that you focus on yourself and control the new, positive aspects of your life. For so long, the focus has been on your parents. Your own childhood wasn't even about you! Now that you are an adult building your own life, you get to decide how to treat yourself and other people. *Isn't this a freeing thought?* As we come to the end of this book, there has been a lot of information thrown at you and much of it may have been hard to digest.

The knowledge of your situation is what will help you break the cycle moving forward. Now that you know what happened during your childhood and why it happened, you can make the decision to focus on yourself and your own children if you have them. There may always be a part of you that will hold some hope that your parents may come around and this is normal. But shifting the focus toward yourself will prevent that hope from growing and it will allow you to look forward to the life that you deserve, free of any abusive cycles.

CHAPTER SUMMARY

- There are many reasons to detach from a relationship, such as physical or verbal abuse, stress or anxiety, and negativity.
- Having a plan in place to deal with boundary violations when they happen (and they will!) can alleviate anxiety. But if your parents continue to push and ignore the boundaries you put in place, there will have to be *consequences*.
- By re-focusing and even changing our expectations, we can begin to better control our own perspective.
- If you feel that you are still stuck in the abuse cycle, always feeling off after interactions with your parents, it may be time to cut them off.

LEAVE A 1-CLICK REVIEW!

I would be incredibly thankful if you could take just 60 seconds to write a brief review on Amazon, even if it's just a few sentences.

Scan the QR code below to leave a quick review!

FINAL WORDS

If you endured emotional abuse at the hands of your emotionally immature parents, you know how strong the *cycle of abuse* can be. Emotionally immature parents prevent their children from having the healthy childhood all children deserve and instead rely on the child to take on the role of the parent. There are four primary types of emotionally immature parents: overly emotional, driven, passive, and rejecting. Each one can be emotionally insensitive, lack empathy for their own children, and blame the child for things that are truly their fault. Another type, perhaps the worst type, is the narcissistic parent. This parent suffers from narcissistic personality disorder and has a deep need for admiration and praise.

You may have found that even now in your adulthood, you still are in denial about what occurred throughout your childhood. Many children often stick up for their abusive parents and do not believe there is anything actually wrong with what is going on in the home. This is because they do not know anything else and they are unable to recognize the *emotional abuse*. Not only this, but they actually become *trauma bonded* to the abuser. This is when they form an unhealthy bond with them over time.

Emotional child abuse takes many forms and it can often be in the form of humiliating the child, blaming the child, not recognizing boundaries, and more. These all greatly affect a child's social, mental, and emotional development. Abuse also has a negative effect on brain structure, decreasing the size of important areas responsible for memory, cognitive performance, stress response, emotions, coordination, and more. *As a child, did you lack confidence and feel unable to reassure yourself? Did you have difficulty controlling your emotions or were often acting out?* These are all common signs of emotional abuse.

The abuse cycle takes place over and over again. As you read through **Chapter Three**: The Emotional Abuse Cycle & Manipulation Tactics, you likely recognized several stages of the cycle and different tactics that your parents may have used to manipulate you. *It is this very pattern that keeps victims trapped in the trauma bond with their parent.* They are desperate to get back to the calm stage when their parents are kind to them once again. But during the incident of abuse, many tactics such as **gaslighting, projecting, and scapegoating** are used to manipulate the child into thinking that they are the one who has done something wrong.

Take a moment as you read this to remind yourself that you have done nothing wrong! So many children of abuse take on misplaced shame and guilt from their childhood that follow them into their adult years. Hopefully, this book has helped those negative feelings to subside a bit and has given you some relief. The feeling you had as a child that something was "off" was right all along. It can be hard for abuse victims to know what they can and can't trust. This is because trauma plays tricks on memory. It typically becomes encoded in the memory, leaving everything else to the side. This makes other details about your childhood blurrier and you may doubt your own perception. But I am here to tell you that I believe you and I understand.

If you are a parent now, then you may be looking to break the toxic cycle of abuse and ensure that you are cultivating a healthy, positive relationship with your children. Being a parent can be a beautiful, difficult, and all-consuming experience. But it is so worth it! *The difference between a mediocre parent and a great parent is that the latter is willing to learn and change for the better.* If you are reading this book, you are already a great parent!

Is there a particular parenting style that you adopt? There are many, such as balanced, neutral, nonrestrictive, strict, and overbearing. Each comes with its own pros and cons and you will have to decide what works best for your family. But what you can definitely do is begin to break the toxic cycle by changing the negative messaging programmed in you by your own parents. You want to strive toward being a **healthy family** instead of a **dysfunctional family**. A dysfunctional family unit is what you likely grew up in as a child with emotionally immature parents. You may have taken on the role of trying to cope with this dysfunctional family dynamic. Perhaps you were **the peacekeeper** and tried to diffuse the chaotic energy or maybe you were **the lost child**, and you stayed quiet to avoid being the next target.

One of the damaging effects of emotionally immature parents is the negative attachment style you learned from them. Several attachment styles such as, **ambivalent, avoidant, and disorganized** are all insecure attachment styles in which the child does not feel safe and secure. Their needs, physical and emotional, are not being met, and therefore they have to adapt on their own. Within your dysfunctional household, you may have felt a great deal of conditional love. It is likely your parents showered you with affection when you were "good" or you did something for them but then suddenly took that affection and attention away from you when they felt like it.

In your own life and with your own children, you can work to prevent these unhealthy attachment styles. You do not want to cultivate a **codependent** relationship with your child. Instead, you want to create a secure attachment in which they feel safe to express their needs, wants, and feelings with you, all while creating their own sense of individuality. Our children are sponges, and the best way for us to ensure the abuse cycle stops is to show them what healthy relationships look like.

Your own healing process from your abusive childhood will take time. Healing doesn't mean you have to change yourself or try to fix your parents. It means that you will have to *repair your reality* and rid yourself of the toxic messages that were fed to you in childhood. In order to cultivate healthier attachment styles, you must tap into the things you love and get to know yourself better! You first have to know what you like, what you care about, and what you stand for.

This will help you to find people who also attach securely.

Ultimately, you must acknowledge your inner child and listen to what it is saying to you. Journaling can be a great way to get all these thoughts down and monitor your own emotional patterns. Therapy and a support group can also help you see your own situation from an outside perspective and give you an opportunity to talk to people who have been through something similar.

If you still have your parents in your life today, you may need to form a *healthy detachment* from them during your healing process. There may still be scars from your childhood and setting healthy boundaries will keep you on the right track. Your parents may not like this, which is okay! You will have to release any expectations you have about them. Your parents are simply who they are and you can only control your reaction to them.

Depending on your situation, it may be necessary for you to cut off your parents from your life, even temporarily. This is not something you should feel guilty about. If there are *consistent boundary violations* and feelings of *emotional drainage*, it's time for you to take a step back and assess whether or not the relationship is worth keeping in your life. Remember, *this is your life now! And it is one that will be free of the toxic abuse cycle.* You can make the decision to stop the toxic messages and show your children what a healthy and happy attachment looks like.

> *"We are all capable of change and growth; we just need to know where to begin."*

— BLAINE LEE PARDOE

Gift for you!

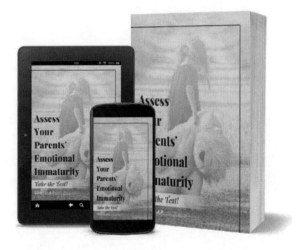

To all my readers, I wish nothing but happiness and peace. To help you identify emotionally immature parents, I created a self-evaluation checklist that points out some of the signs of toxic behavior. Scan this QR code to download it:

REFERENCES

10 moms define motherhood - the washington post. (n.d.). Retrieved December 29, 2021, from https:// www.washingtonpost.com/news/style/wp/2019/05/ 09/feature/the-protector-the-multitasker-the-holder-of-rocks-10-moms-define-motherhood/

10 traits of toxic parents who ruin their children's lives without realizing it. Bright Side - Inspiration. Creativity. Wonder. (2018, May 27). Retrieved December 29, 2021, from https://brightside.me/inspiration-psychology/10-traits-of-toxic-parents-who-ruin-their-childrens-lives-without-realizing-it-518010/

14 signs of psychological and emotional manipulation ... (n.d.). Retrieved December 29, 2021, from https:// www.psychologytoday.com/us/blog/communication-

success/201510/14-signs-psychological-and-emotional-manipulation

5 ways to release your expectations | psychology Today. (n.d.). Retrieved December 29, 2021, from https://www.psychologytoday.com/us/blog/enlightened-living/201108/5-ways-release-your-expectations

American Psychological Association. (n.d.). Apa Dictionary of Psychology. American Psychological Association. Retrieved December 29, 2021, from https://dictionary.apa.org/self

Amy Morin, L. C. S. W. (2021, October 9). 4 types of parenting styles and their effects on kids. Verywell Family. Retrieved December 29, 2021, from https://www.verywellfamily.com/types-of-parenting-styles-1095045

BA, A. U. (n.d.). Cost of growing up in dysfunctional family. ClinMed International Library. Retrieved December 29, 2021, from https://clinmedjournals.org/articles/jfmdp/journal-of-family-medicine-and-disease-prevention-jfmdp-3-059.php?jid=jfmdp

Bomzer, R. (2021, June 25). What does it mean to be a parent? Carved Culture. Retrieved December 29, 2021, from https://www.carvedculture.com/blogs/articles/what-does-it-mean-to-be-a-parent

Cherry, K. (2019, July 17). How attachment theory works. Verywell Mind. Retrieved December 29, 2021, from https://www.verywellmind.com/what-is-attachment-theory-2795337

Cherry, K. (2020, December 9). The structure and levels of the mind according to freud. Verywell Mind. Retrieved December 29, 2021, from https://www.verywellmind.com/the-conscious-and-unconscious-mind-2795946

Cherry, K. (2021, April 25). What is emotional detachment? Verywell Mind. Retrieved December 29, 2021, from https://www.verywellmind.com/what-is-emotional-detachment-5121166

Cherry, K. (n.d.). How cognitive behavior therapy works. Verywell Mind. Retrieved December 29, 2021, from https://www.verywellmind.com/what-is-cognitive-behavior-therapy-2795747

Debra Campbell, P. D. (2021, July 1). How to rewire your brain to have a secure attachment style. mindbodygreen. Retrieved December 29, 2021, from https://www.mindbodygreen.com/articles/how-to-develop-a-secure-attachment-style

Drake, W. (2021, February 4). What is splitting psychology? BetterHelp. Retrieved December 29, 2021, from https://www.betterhelp.com/advice/psychologists/ what-is-splitting-psychology/

Dyke, K. V. (2021, August 20). How to emotionally detach from someone. Psych Central. Retrieved December 29, 2021, from https://psychcentral.com/ lib/the-what-why-when-and-how-of-detaching-from-loved-ones

Elizabeth Earnshaw, L. M. F. T. (2021, June 25). 6 types of boundaries you deserve to have (and how to maintain them). mindbodygreen. Retrieved December 29, 2021, from https://www.mindbodygreen.com/articles/ six-types-of-boundaries-and-what-healthy-boundaries-look-like-for-each

Emotionally immature parents: Signs and how to cope ... (n.d.). Retrieved December 29, 2021, from https:// www.psychologytoday.com/us/blog/mental-wealth/ 202111/emotionally-immature-parents-signs-and-how-cope

Gordon, S. (2021, November 2). Ways to tell if someone is gaslighting you. Verywell Mind. Retrieved December 29, 2021, from https://www.verywellmind.com/is-someone-gaslighting-you-4147470

Gould, W. R. (2020, December 8). What is codependency? Verywell Mind. Retrieved December 29, 2021, from https://www.verywellmind.com/what-is-codependency-5072124

Hax, C. (2016, May 16). If parents won't change, change how you see them. Detroit Free Press. Retrieved December 29, 2021, from https://www.freep.com/story/life/advice/2016/05/16/carolyn-hax-parents-will-change-change-see/84287466/

How to change your attachment style and your relationships ... (n.d.). Retrieved December 29, 2021, from https://www.psychologytoday.com/us/blog/toxic-relationships/202104/how-change-your-attachment-style-and-your-relationships

How to determine the right consequences when setting boundaries. Boundaries Books. (n.d.). Retrieved December 29, 2021, from https://www.boundariesbooks.com/blogs/boundaries-blog/how-to-determine-the-right-consequences-when-setting-boundaries

Kristalyn Salters-Pedneault, P. D. (2021, February 18). Why your whole self feels ashamed but only part of you feels guilty. Verywell Mind. Retrieved December 29, 2021, from https://www.verywellmind.com/what-is-shame-425328

Leonard Holmes, P. D. (2021, November 15). Childhood abuse and neglect actually change brain structure.

Verywell Mind. Retrieved December 29, 2021, from https://www.verywellmind.com/childhood-abuse-changes-the-brain-2330401

Lewis, R. (2020, November 30). Parent codependency: Recognizing the signs. Healthline. Retrieved December 29, 2021, from https://www.healthline.com/health/parenting/parent-codependency

Mark Manson. (2021, September 22). It's not all your parents' fault. Mark Manson. Retrieved December 29, 2021, from https://markmanson.net/parents

Mayo Foundation for Medical Education and Research. (2018, July 6). Post-traumatic stress disorder (PTSD). Mayo Clinic. Retrieved December 29, 2021, from https://www.mayoclinic.org/diseases-conditions/post-traumatic-stress-disorder/expert-answers/trauma-memory/faq-20448198

Mcleod], [S. (1970, January 1). [Sigmund Freud's theories]. What are the most interesting ideas of Sigmund Freud? | Simply Psychology. Retrieved December 29, 2021, from https://www.simplypsychology.org/Sigmund-Freud.html

Nspcc. (n.d.). What is child abuse? NSPCC. Retrieved December 29, 2021, from https://www.nspcc.org.uk/what-is-child-abuse/

Pattemore, C. (2021, June 3). 10 ways to build and preserve better boundaries. Psych Central. Retrieved December 29, 2021, from https://psychcentral.com/lib/10-way-to-build-and-preserve-better-boundaries#10-tips

Person. (2021, October 21). 8 tips for Healing your inner child. Healthline. Retrieved December 29, 2021, from https://www.healthline.com/health/mental-health/inner-child-healing

Raypole, C. (2019, December 13). Grey rock method: 6 tips and Techniques. Healthline. Retrieved December 29, 2021, from https://www.healthline.com/health/grey-rock

Raypole, C. (2019, December 13). Grey rock method: 6 tips and Techniques. Healthline. Retrieved December 29, 2021, from https://www.healthline.com/health/grey-rock#offer-nothing

Sharie Stines, P. D. (2019, May 22). Healing from an emotionally abusive mother. Psych Central. Retrieved December 29, 2021, from https://psychcentral.com/pro/recovery-expert/2019/05/healing-from-an-emotionally-abusive-mother#4

Sharie Stines, P. D. (2019, May 22). Healing from an emotionally abusive mother. Psych Central. Retrieved December 29, 2021, from https://psychcentral.com/

pro/recovery-expert/2019/05/healing-from-an-emotionally-abusive-mother#4

Therapy, H. (2020, March 7). Conditional vs. Unconditional Love. Hudson Therapy Group. Retrieved December 29, 2021, from https://hudsontherapygroup.com/blog/conditional-vs-unconditional-love

Victoria Grande, L. M. H. C. (2021, October 29). Roles in the narcissistic family: The scapegoat child. Psych Central. Retrieved December 29, 2021, from https://psychcentral.com/health/scapegoat-child

Why people abuse. The Hotline. (2021, November 29). Retrieved December 29, 2021, from https://www.thehotline.org/identify-abuse/why-do-people-abuse/

Young, K. (2020b, August 17). Breaking the Cycle of Toxic Parenting – How to Silence Old Toxic Messages for Good. Hey Sigmund. https://www.heysigmund.com/breaking-the-cycle-of-toxic-parenting/

Made in the USA
Middletown, DE
09 June 2023

32304278R00109